Crepe Paper
BLOOMS, BUGS & BUTTERFLIES

Over 20 colourful paper projects
from Miss Petal & Bloom

Eileen Lim

DAVID & CHARLES

www.davidandcharles.com

CONTENTS

Introduction

Dear paper flower lover,

Thank you for purchasing this book! You are holding in your hands my ode to crafting, a celebration of the handmade, and an invitation for you to explore the exciting world of crepe paper flowers.

Each bloom and bug in this book has gone through many incarnations and lots of trial and error over the years. My creations are not necessarily the most refined, botanically accurate, or true to size, but that's what I love about creating from scratch – there aren't any rules! With five years of flower-making under my belt, I am delighted to share my secrets and tips to crafting a whimsical handmade garden.

One of my goals for this book is to reveal techniques for crafting colourful blooms and bugs without breaking the bank – which is why I focus solely on one kind of crepe paper. You may, of course, choose to use other crepe paper alternatives, but I do love 180gsm Italian crepe paper and I hope you'll fall in love with it too!

Whether you're a beginner or an experienced paper florist, I recommend reading through the Basic Techniques chapter before starting on a project. For new crafters, you might want to practise these techniques on your own, as this will help your hands become familiar with the motions of manipulating crepe paper.

Each project has a difficulty rating from one to five, yet please do not be intimidated by this number. Projects ranked five out of five do not mean that they are super advanced and cannot be accomplished by beginners. I have added this rating more as a helpful guide in estimating the amount of time and effort that you will need for the project, since most of the techniques you will encounter are fundamentally the same across the board.

All templates are found in the back of this book, but I do suggest hopping online at www.davidandcharles.com for the printable versions for convenience.

While this book has step-by-step instructions to guide you, I encourage you to step outside the box – don't be afraid to experiment and put your own stamp on your creations! The possibilities are endless, and at the end of the day, there is truly no right or wrong way to craft a bloom, bug or butterfly. I want you to know that you have a cheerleader in me, and I hope these pages offer you much joy and inspiration. If you take away nothing else from this book, know that there's an artist within you, and your hands have an amazing ability to create wonderful things.

Keep Blooming,

Eileen

Tools and Materials

You don't need any complicated or expensive materials for projects in this book, as most can be sourced from your local craft store or online. In this section, I share more about my favourite crepe paper and its qualities. I've also included a general list of important tools and materials, though you'll find more specific lists within the projects themselves.

ITALIAN CREPE PAPER

All projects in this book are crafted from 180gsm Italian crepe paper, and I purchase my rolls from Italian manufacturer Cartotecnica Rossi. I use the thickest weight of crepe paper as it has the most stretch, which equates to more crafting possibilities.

Colour codes quoted in this book are all based on Cartotecnica Rossi's catalogue and you can order crepe paper rolls through their online store. Do note that I've renamed the colours in the projects to make life easier, so they may not match the colour names on the online store.

While you can find a range of crepe papers on the market, do note that their qualities (such as stretchability, strength and range of colours) vary according to their weights and manufacturer. To allow your projects to last longer, I encourage you to invest in higher quality crepe papers.

CREPE PAPER GRAIN

1a. The grain refers to the vertical creases found on the rough surface of our Italian crepe paper. They are formed when multiple layers of tissue paper are compressed together during the production process. Without this grain, Italian crepe paper would not have such amazing stretchability and malleability. It's important to take note of the direction of the grain as it will indicate the direction for cutting and sculpting.

CREPE PAPER SCRAPS

1b. Scraps can come in handy for smaller blooms and fillers. For instance, they can be scrunched up and moulded into round shapes for flower buds or bugs' bodies. I keep my scraps in boxes sorted according to their colours.

FLORIST WIRE

2a. The thickness of florist wire is indicated by its gauge. The smaller the number, the thicker the wire. I work primarily with five gauges: #18, #20, #22, #24 and #26. I use the thickest wire for flower stalks and the thinnest wire for leaves, bugs' feelers, etc.

PRE-WRAPPED #18 FLORIST WIRE

2b. For flower stalks, I use pre-wrapped #18 florist wire – these come wrapped in paper or cloth and measure 3mm (⅛in) or more in width. Having them pre-wrapped saves me time and as they're thicker and stronger, they can support larger flowerheads. I purchase them from my local craft store or from online retailers. If you're unable to find these, you could wrap your normal #18 wire by hand with multiple strips of stretched green crepe paper.

SCISSORS

3. Invest in a good pair of scissors that will last you through years of flower-making. Pick a pair that has a comfortable grip and sharp blades, as this will help you cut through multiple layers of crepe paper easily in one go.

PLIERS AND WIRE CUTTERS

4. Most long-nose pliers conveniently come with wire-cutting blades above the pivot point, allowing you to both trim and bend wires.

PAINTBRUSHES

5. I use flat or angled brushes for blending soft pastels, and fine-pointed, round brushes for painting more intricate details.

WATERCOLOUR PAINTS

6. For painting crepe paper, I prefer watercolour paints in tube form as they have a richer intensity compared to watercolour pans.

FOAM BALLS AND SHAPES

7. These foam pieces come in particularly handy when building the foundations of different blooms and bugs. The most common shapes I use are the 2cm (¾in) and 1.5cm (⅝in) round balls.

WOODEN SKEWERS AND DOWELS

8. These are simple yet so useful. I use them to curl my petals and to spread white craft glue when laminating crepe paper strips.

MINI HOT GLUE GUN AND GLUE STICKS

9. Using hot glue is my default method for gluing my crepe paper projects. I prefer using a mini hot glue gun rather than a full-size gun as it's easier to handle. What I love most about hot glue is that it dries quickly and it won't create a soggy mess. Moreover, hot glue is not permanent, which means you can make corrections by carefully peeling off the glued-on component even after the glue has dried. I like to give my glue gun a good three to five minutes to warm up before I begin a project.

To protect yourself from burns, please handle your hot glue gun with care and avoid touching the metal tip. A glue gun of good quality should not leak excessively when not in use.

Glue strings are inevitable and can be easily removed. I use a lint roller to remove any trailing glue strings.

WHITE CRAFT GLUE

10. White craft glue is great for gluing processes that require close contact with our fingers (like wrapping and making leaves), as well as steps that require a large spread of glue (such as laminating crepe paper strips). Choose a glue that dries clear and has a small nozzle for precise application. Most importantly, make sure your white glue does not discolour your crepe paper.

WOODEN PEGS

11. Wooden pegs are a cheap and easy way to organise your crepe paper stacks and templates. I have a box full of templates and I use wooden pegs to keep template cut-outs from the same project together.

SOFT PASTELS

12. Soft pastels are my favourite way of adding colour onto crepe paper surfaces. They blend easily with a paintbrush, allowing me to create subtle ombre finishes on my crepe paper components.

ADDITIONAL TOOLS

Permanent ink markers: I often use these in maroon and black for adding details, especially for wing patterns or spot patterns on blooms. Markers with fine brush tips are ideal.

Acrylic paint: For projects in this book, you'll only need white acrylic paint. We'll use it for the butterflies, moths, foxgloves and anemones.

Bone folder: These are great for scoring and defining lines or veins, especially for the wings of our crepe paper bugs.

Needle: A simple, yet useful item when adding feelers and legs to our bugs.

Calyx (made of sepals)

ANATOMY OF A FLOWER

In the projects, I sometimes refer to specific parts of the flowers using botanical terms. Take a look at the image below if you ever need a reminder about the names of these parts and where the pieces are roughly positioned.

Leaf

Petiole

Carpels (in green)

Stamen (in yellow)

Petals

Leaf stalk

Main stalk

Basic Techniques

These techniques are used throughout the projects in this book. At the beginning of each project you will find a list of techniques and can refer back to this section for a refresher at any time.

CUTTING

1. It's best to cut crepe paper with a sharp pair of scissors, working with or against the grain. You can cut through multiple layers at once to save time.

Each template supplied includes a line to indicate the direction the grain of the crepe paper should follow. For most petals, the template is aligned with the grain running vertically, but check carefully as some petals and leaves need to be aligned diagonally.

I cut my petals using the accordion fold technique. For this method, prepare a long strip of crepe paper following the height of the template. Place your template at one end of the strip and make accordion folds (i.e. a series of alternate folds or pleats, in a zigzag pattern) behind the template. This will result in a neat folded stack, which will allow you to cut multiple petals in one go.

STRETCHING

2. Stretching out 180gsm crepe paper not only thins the paper and smooths out the grain, but it also doubles the surface area we can work with.

I generally use stretched crepe paper for fringed stamens, but also for thinner, lightweight petals and leaves that do not require a lot of sculpting.

I work each strip by pulling out both ends across a smooth table surface to achieve a nice even stretch. Stretching the paper on a table surface like this (as opposed to pulling it in the air) will help prevent the paper from warping.

While stretched crepe paper will certainly not be as flexible as it was in its original form, it is usually still slightly malleable and can be gently cupped or curled (see *Cupping* and *Curling*).

Be aware, though, that all crepe paper in my projects is unstretched unless specified in that project or technique.

FRINGING

3. Fringing means snipping into the crepe paper to create thin, even cuts along the length of your crepe paper strip, parallel to the grain.

It is important to leave a margin at the base of your strip for glue application.

You can fold your strip in half widthways to fringe more efficiently, but remember to unfold and check for any areas you might have missed.

1.

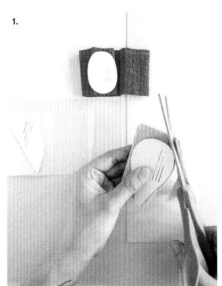

2.

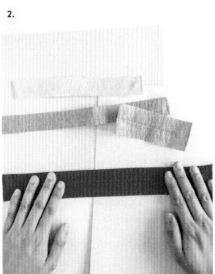

3.

CUPPING

1. Cupping describes the technique of sculpting flat crepe paper petals into three-dimensional concave shapes that resemble bowls.

To cup a petal, first pinch it at either side of the belly (or widest part) of the shape using your thumbs and index fingers as shown.

Pull the two edges outwards and towards you. Stretch that belly until you have a wide, concave shape. The top and bottom of the petal should be left unstretched.

CURLING

2. Curling usually requires the help of a curling tool such as a wooden skewer or pencil to create a distinct curl on the crepe paper surface.

For loose curls, simply press your petal between the tool and your fingers, then drag it across the upper portion of your petal once or twice until a curl forms. This method is quite similar to the way you would curl ribbon with the blade of a pair of scissors.

For a tighter curl, wrap your petal tightly around your curling tool and roll it up, working downwards. Slide your curling tool out without unrolling the paper and a defined curl will remain in the paper.

WRAPPING

3. Once you have completed your flower head, you need to wrap the stalk. Even though we use *pre-wrapped* #18 wire for stalks, I still like to wrap them so that the colours match (the green of the original wire usually doesn't match the green of the crepe). You can use floral tape but I prefer to use crepe paper so that the colours and textures are consistent throughout. Wrapping the stalk also allows you to add your leaves.

Always use white craft glue and apply a thin line all the way along the narrow stretched crepe paper strips for wrapping (see *Stretching*).

Starting at the bottom of your flower head, wrap the pre-stretched crepe paper strip tightly around the calyx (see *Anatomy of a Flower*), pinching it tightly before continuing. With one hand pulling the strip and angling it diagonally downwards, and the other holding the flower stem, twist the stem so that the strip continues to wrap around until you reach the end of the wire. If one strip is not sufficient, simply continue with a new strip.

Snip off any excess at the end with sharp scissors.

BOW TIES

I have taken to calling this effect the bow tie technique as the knotted strip resembles a cute bow tie. I use it for creating small buds or carpels (see *Anatomy of a Flower*) and to cover the tips of my florist wire.

4. Prepare a thin rectangular strip of unstretched crepe paper. Make a twist at the centre of the strip by holding it at both ends and flipping one end backwards.

5. Cup and stretch each end of the bow tie towards you as shown.

6. Bend the two ends towards each other to create a rounded, full tip.

7. For carpels, glue the two stretched, wider ends of the bow tie together, so that the twisted portion forms the tip of the carpel. For wrapping wire tips, position the twist right at the end of the wire and glue each flap down around the wire, making sure the tip of the wire is tightly covered.

It's a good idea to practise all of these techniques before you start the projects to ensure you are familiar with them and can control the results.

When wrapping, don't apply too much glue, as the excess might result in a soggy mess. A thin, sparse line of glue down the centre of the strip is sufficient.

LAMINATING

Lamination is an extremely useful technique for adding a polished, refined look to your blooms. I use laminated crepe paper when I need smooth, hardy petals that are still stretchable and malleable.

1. Cut a length of crepe paper that's the same height as your template and stretch it out fully (see *Stretching*).

2. Focusing on the right-hand half of the strip, apply white craft glue – I like to apply it in thin, checkered lines. Spread the glue evenly across the strip using a wooden skewer.

3. Fold the strip in half widthways to glue the two halves together. Press down firmly for a nice, smooth, even surface.

4. If the laminated strip is too wet to handle, leave it to dry slightly before cutting out your petals. However, I recommend cutting and sculpting your petals before the glue completely hardens and stiffens the paper.

MAKING LEAVES

When making leaves from crepe paper, we want to take advantage of the grain to mimic the leaf veins. For some projects, this means that instead of cutting out the full leaf shape, we do it in two halves.

5. Cut a crepe paper strip so that the width matches the diagonal height of your chosen leaf template. Stretch fully (see *Stretching*). Make an accordion fold (see *Cutting*) and cut the folded stack diagonally in half.

6. Position your template on top of a triangular stack, with the longest edge of the leaf template aligning with the diagonal edge of the paper and the grain matching the direction of the leaf veins. Cut out the half-leaf shape through all the layers of paper.

7. Lay out the separate leaf halves in the same direction and apply a line of white craft glue along their straight edges.

8. To make a complete leaf, place a piece of #26 wire along the glue line on one leaf half to make the leaf stalk. Flip over the second leaf half to reverse the grain and glue both pieces together, overlapping slightly to cover the wire.

9. Trim away any protruding parts with scissors, then leave to dry (see Tip for extra advice).

10. You may choose to wrap (see *Wrapping*) a short portion of the leaf stalk below the leaf with narrow stretched crepe paper in a matching green to create a short petiole (see *Anatomy of a Flower*). To make a branch, simply wrap multiple wired leaves onto a longer piece of wire (the central wire could be of a thicker gauge, I recommend using #24 or #22 wires).

11. For added dimension, flute your leaves (i.e. add grooves or furrows) by pinching along the edges with your fingertips and gently pulling in opposite directions.

12. For realistic-looking leaves, rub browns or yellows along the edges using soft pastels. Carefully blend the colours into the paper using a small paintbrush.

We will use the Making Leaves technique for all bloom projects, so be sure to refer back here regularly.

Try playing around with different leaf styles. For certain leaves, you may like to trim jagged edges along the sides of your leaves with sharp scissors.

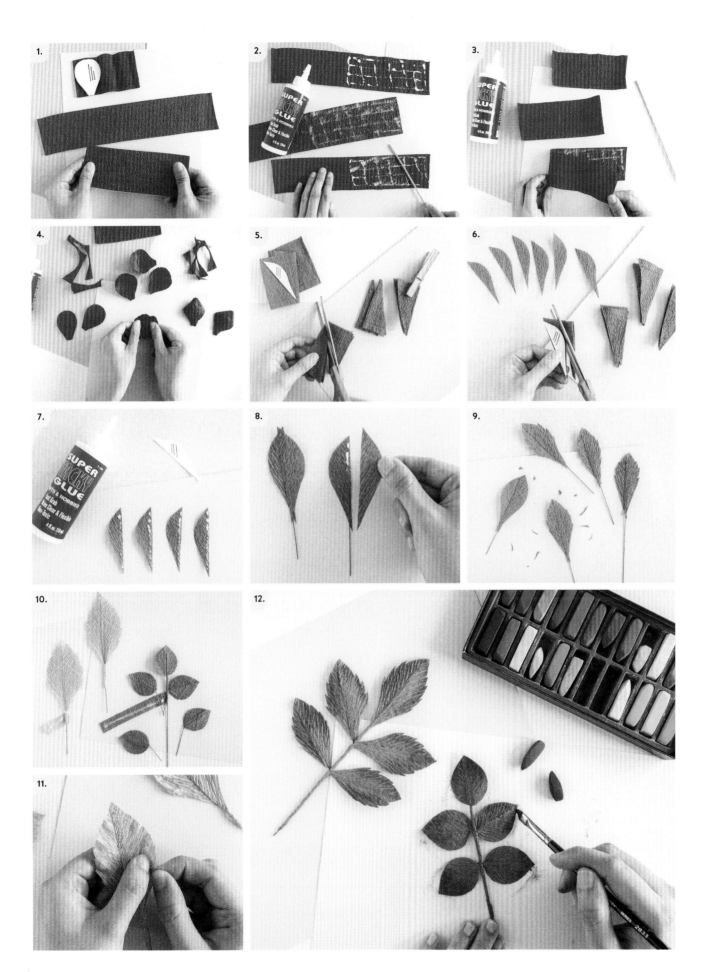

Blooms

BLOOMS

Sunflower

DIFFICULTY

I don't think you'll find a bloom more cheerful than a sunflower! I've made multiple versions of this flower, yet I have to admit that this one right here – with its fluffy centre and short, plump petals – is my absolute favourite. On a botanical note, I must mention that sunflowers are actually composite flowers, meaning they're made up of hundreds of smaller ray and disc florets. However, to simplify matters, I'll refer to the ray florets as petals and the disc florets as the sunflower centre.

YOU WILL NEED

CREPE PAPER
- Yellow #576
- Black #602
- Dark Brown #568
- Light Green #562

OTHER MATERIALS
- Pre-wrapped #18 wire
- #26 wire
- Wooden skewer
- Scissors and wire cutters
- Mini hot glue gun
- White craft glue

TEMPLATES
Centre: SUN1, SUN2
Petals: SUN3
Calyx: SUN4, SUN5
Leaves: SUN6

MAIN TECHNIQUES
Bow Ties, Cupping, Curling, Fringing, Laminating

PETALS

1. Prepare laminated Yellow crepe paper, then cut around 36 petals from it using template SUN3.

2. Cup each petal across its widest point or belly.

3. To enhance the structure of each petal, pinch the base of the petal from the back. This should create a crease in the middle of your petal. Add hot glue in the crease to seal it in place.

4. With a wooden skewer, curl the tip of the petal away from you.

SUNFLOWER CENTRE

5. From Dark Brown crepe paper, cut four rectangles using template SUN2. Stretch each rectangle, fold it in half and fringe along the *unfolded* edge, with the fringe not longer than a third of the original width.

6. From Black crepe paper, cut three rectangles using template SUN1. Stretch each rectangle, fold it in half, and this time fringe along the *folded* edge, again cutting down to about a third of the width.

7. To add volume to the centre, bunch up the Dark Brown fringe strips and twist them in thick bundles before unravelling them again. This helps to create a frizzy effect on the outer layers of the sunflower centre.

ASSEMBLY

8. Cover the tip of your pre-wrapped #18 wire with Black crepe paper using the bow tie technique. Position the top of your strip at the same level as the tip of your wrapped wire, and wrap on the first Black fringed strip around the wire (with the fringe at the top) using hot glue. Repeat for the remaining two Black fringed strips.

9. Next, glue on the four Dark Brown fringed strips using hot glue, again wrapping them strip by strip with the fringe at the top. As the Dark Brown strips are taller, they should protrude above the Black centre.

10. Once the sunflower centre is complete, start attaching the petals individually using hot glue. I generally prefer to attach nine petals first, gluing them as evenly spaced as possible.

11. Proceed to glue on the remaining petals in approximately three more layers of nine petals each. If you get confused about where to place your petals, you can view the sunflower from the side profile – the brown gaps are helpful indicators for where you can attach your remaining petals.

12. When all the brown gaps from the side profile are filled up, switch to a top-down view and check for any remaining gaps. Keep attaching petals until you achieve an even ring.

13. For the calyx, cut six pieces each of SUN4 and SUN5 from Light Green crepe paper. Cup each SUN4 and SUN5 and hot glue them in two layers onto the underside of the flowerhead, starting with the bigger SUN4s for the first layer, and the smaller SUN5s for the outermost layer. The two layers of sepals should fully cover the underside of the sunflower centre.

14. Add leaves (see *Making Leaves*) with the help of template SUN6 and attach them to the stalk with stretched Light Green crepe paper strips (see *Wrapping*). I like to flute my sunflower leaves for added texture (see *Making Leaves* for how to flute).

1.

2.

3.

4.

5.

6.

7.

8.

9.

10.

11.

12.

13.

I've suggested making 36 petals, but I'm never consistent with this number, so feel free to use more or fewer petals.

14.

Rose

DIFFICULTY

My formula for this classic rose is simple, yet the tricky bit lies in mastering the sculpting techniques when forming the petals. Sculpting crepe paper can be a subtle skill, and it is hard to describe the exact amount of pressure or stretch needed. So, if you find that your rose petals do not look exactly like mine, do not fear! Just keep practising and allow your fingers to grow more comfortable with the crepe paper. With time, curling and cupping will become second nature to you.

YOU WILL NEED

CREPE PAPER
- Red Velvet #586
- Forest Green #561

OTHER MATERIALS
- Pre-wrapped #18 wire
- #26 wire
- 2cm (¾in) foam ball
- Wooden skewer
- Scissors and wire cutters
- Mini hot glue gun
- White craft glue

TEMPLATES
Petals: RO1, RO2
Leaves: RO3

MAIN TECHNIQUES
Cupping, Curling

PETALS

1. Cut 13 large petals, using template RO2, from Red Velvet crepe paper and cup all of them at their bellies to create wide, concave petals.

2. For each RO2 petal, create two tight diagonal curls along the tip of the petal. To do so, position the wooden skewer at a diagonal (45-degree angle) behind the top right corner of the petal. Wrap that corner around the wooden skewer and roll downwards, towards the back of the petal. Repeat on the left side. The rounded tip should now be curled into a pyramid-shaped tip.

3. Cut three small dome-shaped petals (RO1). For just one RO1, stretch it out slightly to expand its surface area, and create one tight diagonal curl towards yourself on the upper right corner of the petal, again using a wooden skewer. This will form the centre swirl for our rose.

4. For the remaining two RO1 petals, gently curl the top edges of the petals backwards.

ROSE CENTRE

5. Using hot glue, attach a 2cm (¾in) foam ball onto the pre-wrapped #18 wire. Take the RO1 petal with the single diagonal curl and hot glue its lower corner onto the foam ball, positioning the curl directly above the foam ball.

6. Pull the other corner of the petal around the foam ball until it overlaps the curled portion. Make sure that this is a tight wrap that creates a sharp narrow cone shape with a tiny round hole at the tip. Once you're happy with the look of the centre swirl, glue down the uncurled edge to secure it in place.

7. Hot glue the two remaining RO1 petals onto the front and back of the swirled petal.

LARGE PETALS

8. Attach all of the large RO2 petals using hot glue in the following three layers, with each layer completing a full round around the rose centre. The first layer is a round of three petals (see Tip).

9. For the second layer, attach five RO2 petals in a round.

10. For the last five petals, stretch them first by gently tugging them at their sides. This makes the petals wider and helps differentiate between the second and third layers of petals. After stretching them out, glue them on as the final layer.

ASSEMBLY

11. For the calyx, cut five to six long, thin triangles from Forest Green crepe paper and hot glue them onto the underside of your flowerhead.

12. For rose leaves, use template RO3 and Forest Green crepe paper, and make three small leaves for each single leaf stalk (see *Making Leaves*). Wrap the rose stalk with stretched Forest Green crepe paper and add your leaf stalks along the way (see *Wrapping*).

When adding a layer of petals, avoid gluing them directly one behind the other. Aim to attach them in between the gaps created by the previous layer of petals.

ROSE

Simple Peony

DIFFICULTY

The name says it all – this peony is one of the simplest flowers to make in the book! It also happens to be one of the very first flowers I made when I discovered crepe paper flowers, and I've stuck with the exact same formula and template since then. I often teach this flower to beginners as the simple peony covers almost all of the basic flower-making techniques without the stress of having too many petals and components. If you want fluffier blooms, feel free to add more petals.

YOU WILL NEED

CREPE PAPER
- Baby Pink #549
- Yellow #576
- Light Green #562
- Dark Green #591

OTHER MATERIALS
- Pre-wrapped #18 wire
- #26 wire
- Thick curling tool (such as a pen or marker)
- Scissors and wire cutters
- Mini hot glue gun
- White craft glue

TEMPLATES
Stamen: SP1

Carpels: SP2

Petals: SP3

Sepals: SP4

Leaves: SP5

MAIN TECHNIQUES
Bow Ties, Cupping, Curling, Fringing

PETALS

1. Cut 12 petals in Baby Pink using template SP3.

2. Create a loose curl on the upper half of each petal by wrapping the tip around a pen or marker. I find it easiest to do this on a table, letting the petal curl around the marker until the petal's tip touches the middle of the petal.

3. After curling, cup each petal to create wide, fat, concave petals.

STAMEN AND CARPELS

4. Cut one rectangle from Yellow crepe paper using template SP1. Stretch and fringe this strip.

5. Cut four rectangles in Light Green for the carpels using SP2 and prepare them using the bow tie technique. Use one to cover the tip of your pre-wrapped #18 wire. Glue the ends of the other three together and attach them to the wrapped tip of your carpels, using hot glue.

6. To form the stamen, apply hot glue at the base of the Yellow fringed strip and wrap it around the carpels.

7. Once the stamen is fully attached, use your fingers to spread out the fringe so that it forms an even circle around the carpels.

ASSEMBLY

8. Apply hot glue at the base of each petal and attach it to the stamen. I align the bottom edge of the petal with the bottom edge of the stamen. Use three petals for the first layer.

9. For the second layer of petals, glue four petals in a round. Avoid attaching petals directly back-to-back.

10. Attach the remaining five petals as your last layer.

11. For the calyx, cut three to four sepals (SP4) from stretched Dark Green crepe paper and glue to the base of your flowerhead.

12. Wrap the rest of your stalk with stretched Dark Green crepe paper and attach two or more leaves (SP5) along the stalk (see *Making Leaves* and *Wrapping*).

I tend to make these with all petals in the same colour but blending petals of different colours would look great too.

1.

2.

3.

4.

5.

6.

7.

8.

9.

10.

11.

12.

SIMPLE PEONY

Coral Charm Peony

DIFFICULTY

True to its name, the irresistible fluffiness of the coral charm peony makes it a very popular flower among florists and artists alike. For beginners, I recommend completing the simple peony first before venturing on to make these beauties, as we do borrow many elements from the former to make the latter. While colouring the petals is optional, I find that this step creates a lovely yet subtle, faded look to the petal tips, which ultimately adds to the realism of the overall bloom.

YOU WILL NEED

CREPE PAPER

- Rusty Red #17A6, plus red scraps
- Yellow #576
- Light Green #562
- Dark Green #591

OTHER MATERIALS

- Pre-wrapped #18 wire
- #26 wire
- Soft pastels in white
- Paintbrush
- Wooden dowel
- Scissors and wire cutters
- Mini hot glue gun
- White craft glue

TEMPLATES

Petals: CCP1, CCP2, CCP3

Stamen: SP1

Carpels: SP2

Sepals: SP4

Leaves: CCP4

MAIN TECHNIQUES

Bow Ties, Cupping, Curling, Fringing, Stretching

PETALS

1. From the Rusty Red crepe paper, cut seven small petals (template CCP1), seven medium petals (CCP2) and 20 large petals (CCP3). For each petal, rub on soft pastels in white around the tips. Brush to blend.

2. Create a loose curl on each petal by running a wooden dowel against the upper half of the petal.

3. Cup each petal to create wide, curved petals.

4. For variation, cut small, narrow triangular slits along the tip of some of your petals. I like to add this detail to about a third of my petals.

STAMEN AND CARPELS

5. Cut two rectangles from Yellow crepe paper, using template SP1. Stretch and fringe both strips.

6. To create a more haphazard look to your stamen, twist bundles of the fringed portion together before unravelling them.

7. Prepare four bow ties in Light Green (SP2). Wrap one around the tip of the pre-wrapped #18 wire.

8. For the remaining bow ties, prepare three small rectangular pieces in any shade of red (I've used Red Velvet #586, but you can use any red scraps). Twist one end and stretch out the other end to make a tiny flag shape.

9. Glue the twisted end of a red flag inside each bow tie, ensuring the top of the flag sticks out from the knotted middle. Glue the flaps of the bow tie together at the base to form a carpel.

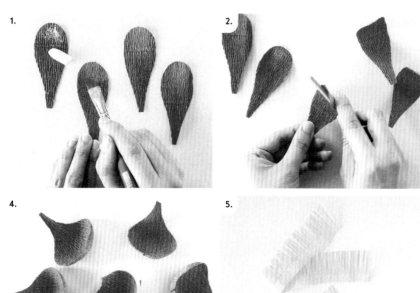

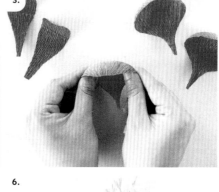

ASSEMBLY

10. Attach the three carpels around the tip of the pre-wrapped #18 wire from step 7. Wrap the two Yellow fringed strips around the carpels.

11. For the first layer of petals, glue seven small petals (CCP1) around the stamen, aligning the bases of the petals with the base of the stamen.

12. For the second layer of petals, glue on a round of seven medium-sized petals (CCP2).

13. Glue on five large petals (CCP3) in a round for the third layer.

14. Group the remaining large petals into five sets of three. Glue each set together at the base in a fanned-out shape. This technique is great for maximising the fluffiness of the peony.

15. For the fourth layer of petals, glue on the five fanned-out petal trios to complete the final round.

16. Glue four or five sepals (SP4) onto the underside of the peony flower head as shown. Wrap the main stalk with stretched Dark Green crepe paper, adding leaves (CCP4) along the way (see *Wrapping* and *Making Leaves*).

10.

11.

12.

13.

For a more natural look, position your petals in a random fashion - they do not need to be evenly spaced out as that will make it appear too uniform.

16.

14.

15.

Ranunculus

DIFFICULTY

With a perfectly round appearance, the Ranunculus is known for having multiple, tight layers of thin, delicate petals. If this intimidates you, fret not, I'm here to assure you that my version is straightforward and not too challenging. In fact, my formula for this bloom has remained almost unchanged since I first made it in 2016. Moreover, it is such a useful bloom to have in your arsenal, especially as its petite size makes it a beautiful filler flower for large bouquets.

YOU WILL NEED

CREPE PAPER
- Orange #610
- Yellow #576
- Light Green #562

OTHER MATERIALS
- Pre-wrapped #18 wire
- #26 wire
- 2cm (¾in) foam ball
- Scissors and wire cutters
- Mini hot glue gun
- White craft glue

TEMPLATES
Petals: RAN1, RAN2
Leaves: RAN3

MAIN TECHNIQUES
Cupping

PETALS

1. Cut ten small petals using template RAN1 and 15 large petals using template RAN2. Cut the smaller petals in the darker shade (in this case, Orange) and the large petals in the lighter shade (Yellow). Cup all 25 petals at their bellies.

2. Set aside five large petals, we won't need them until step 9. For the remaining small petals and ten large petals, make a snip at the middle of each petal, up to the centre of the petal. The resulting shape looks a bit like a fortune cookie.

3. Grab the two bottom corners created by the slit, and pull one flap over the other, making an overlap. Add hot glue to this overlapped area to glue the two bottoms together. This tightening technique helps to create a more defined cupped shape for the petals.

FLOWER CENTRE

4. Hot glue a 2cm (¾in) foam ball onto a pre-wrapped #18 wire. Cover the tip of the foam ball with a small square piece of stretched crepe in Light Green, securing it with hot glue.

5. Cut five small, curved triangles from stretched Light Green crepe paper. I like to cut these freehand, as you don't need to have them all precisely the same size.

6. Glue these five shapes around the tip, with their sides touching. As these shapes are so small, you can glue these on with hot glue or white glue, whichever you prefer. This should result in a tiny star shape right in the middle.

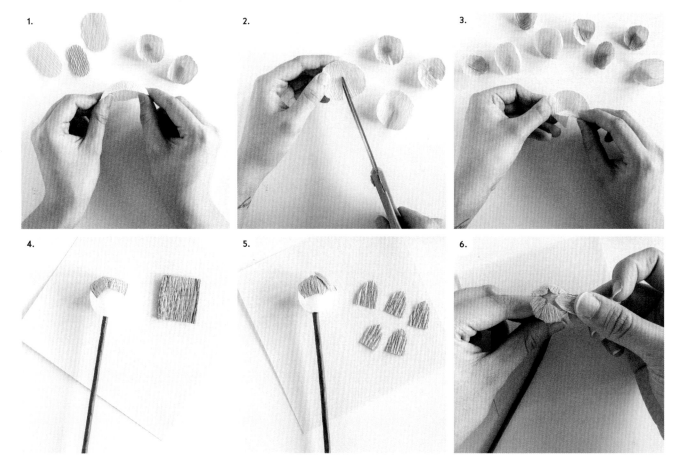

ASSEMBLY

7. For the first layer of petals, apply hot glue to the base of each petal and then glue on five small petals in a round, making sure each petal is cupped snugly around the foam ball. The overlapped portion of your petals (created in step 3) should always be the bottom. Repeat with five small petals for layer 2.

8. For layers 3 and 4 of the petals, glue on five large, tightened petals in a round for each layer.

9. For layer 5, bring back the five large un-tightened petals that we set aside at step 2. Glue them on to make the final round of petals.

10. At this stage, after all the petals are attached, I like to gently push back the outer round of petals to add volume to the bloom.

11. For the calyx, glue on three rounded triangles from stretched Light Green. Again, I cut these freehand and attach them on with hot glue.

12. With the help of template RAN3, make leaves from stretched Light Green. Wrap these to the main stalk using stretched Light Green crepe paper strips to complete your bloom (see *Making Leaves* and *Wrapping*).

To blend any two colours in a bloom, use one darker colour for the smaller petals and another lighter colour for the larger ones.

7.

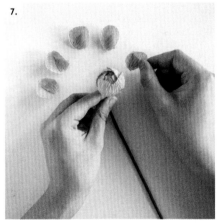

8.

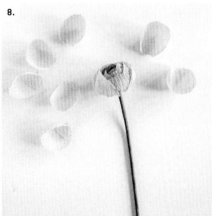

9.

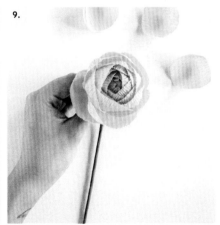

10.

11.

12.

BLOOMS

Dahlia

DIFFICULTY

With more than 50 petals, this dahlia can take a while to make, yet it is no doubt one of my favourites in the book. The fun bit comes in blending the colours. My trick for creating a natural-looking ombre effect is to distribute two shades across successive petal layers in a completely random and unpredictable manner. I am biased towards this beautiful blend of peach shades, but you are welcome to use a single shade or experiment with other shades as well.

YOU WILL NEED

CREPE PAPER
- Dusty Peach #17A2
- Light Peach #17A5
- Dark Green #591

OTHER MATERIALS
- Pre-wrapped #18 wire
- #26 wire
- 2cm (¾in) foam ball
- Wooden skewer
- Scissors and wire cutters
- Mini hot glue gun
- White craft glue

TEMPLATES
Dahlia Centre: DA1, DA2
Petals: DA3, DA4, DA5, DA6
Leaves: DA7

MAIN TECHNIQUES
Cupping, Curling, Laminating

PREPARING YOUR PETALS

1. From laminated crepe paper in your chosen colours (see *Laminating*), cut at least 11 of DA3, 11 of DA4, 12 of DA5 and 24 of DA6. If you would like an ombre effect, cut more of the small petals in the darker shade, and more large petals in the lighter shade. Cup all petals at their bellies to form nice concave petals. I recommend having extra petals on hand.

DAHLIA CENTRE

2. For the dahlia centre, cut two of DA1 and one of DA2. Curl their tips towards you with a wooden skewer.

3. Use hot glue to attach a 2cm (¾in) foam ball to the tip of the pre-wrapped #18 wire and wrap the head of the foam ball with stretched crepe paper in the same shade as your lighter petals.

4. Apply hot glue along the base of each of the two pieces of DA1 and wrap them around the foam ball, followed by DA2, with the curled petals pointing inwards.

5. We will use our DA3s (from step 1) for our first round of rolled petals. To create a rolled, curled-in petal (like a cannoli shell), I draw a line of hot glue near the base and fold in the sides, ensuring the sides overlap. You can also pinch the tips for a pointed look to your petals.

6. Next, glue the DA3 petals around the dahlia centre with hot glue until you complete a round. I like to trim some of my DA3 petals smaller for a more random mix of sizes, just for this round of petals.

SMALL AND MEDIUM PETALS

7. For each of DA4 and DA5 petals, fold in the sides on the lower half of each petal and glue them down with hot glue. This again helps to create a rolled or curled-in effect to each petal and adds volume to the overall dahlia. Pinch the tips of each petal as well.

8. Attach the 11 DA4 petals in a round, followed by the 12 DA5 petals. Remember to mix in your two shades of petals in a random fashion. Make sure the petals are glued tightly next to each other with no obvious gaps.

LARGE PETALS

9. Split the 24 large DA6 petals into two groups of 12 each. Repeat step 7 for only one group of 12 DA6 petals.

10. At this stage, you can also use your fingers to gently sculpt or curl back the tips of these 12 large petals with your fingers. This is to anticipate the final, outermost layer of petals, which will be fully curled downwards.

11. Hot glue this first group of DA6 petals on, positioning them slightly lower than the previous layers so that they wrap around the wire stalk for extra support.

12. For the remaining DA6 petals, leave the base of each petal unfolded. With their cupped bellies facing away from you, twist the tips in various directions to create wavy petals.

13. Glue the final 12 petals using hot glue as the last layer, ensuring that their tips curl downwards.

14. To complete the dahlia, add the calyx (five to six rounded Dark Green triangles), wrap the stalk with stretched Dark Green crepe paper, and attach leaves that have been cut using template DA7 (see *Wrapping* and *Making Leaves*).

An ombre effect is created by using smaller, darker petals around the centre of the bloom, and gradually adding more petals in a lighter shade for each successive layer.

BLOOMS

Oriental Poppy

DIFFICULTY

Boasting vivid colours, crinkly petals and fuzzy centres, these oriental poppies may look messy and wild, but I love them all the more because of it. You can mix and match different colours for the different components, plus the crinkling of the petals is a super-fun step that helps us achieve a wonderful, wrinkled texture for our petals. To add even more whimsy, I usually make these poppies with long, winding stalks (and no leaves) and display them in tall, narrow vases.

YOU WILL NEED

CREPE PAPER

- Magenta #572
- Black #602
- White #600
- Light Green #562
- Wine #588

OTHER MATERIALS

- Pre-wrapped #18 wire
- 2cm (¾in) foam ball
- Scissors and wire cutters
- Mini hot glue gun
- White craft glue

TEMPLATES

Petals: OP1, OP2, OP3
Stamen: OP4

MAIN TECHNIQUES

Fluting, Fringing, Stretching

PETALS

1. Cut three small poppy petals of template OP1 and five large petals of OP2 from stretched Magenta crepe paper. Next, cut out eight petals (OP3) from stretched Black crepe paper. Spread a thin layer of white craft glue on the back of each OP3 piece and attach it to the middle of each poppy petal with both bases aligned.

2. To create that wrinkled texture, crinkle all petals by twisting them into rolled up strips, similar to how you would wring a towel.

3. Gently unfurl the petal – you should find it all crinkly and wavy. You can also gently flute the top border of the petal to create even more creases (see Making Leaves for how to flute).

4. I like to pinch in the bases of all petals in order to taper down the base. This will make it easier to glue the petals onto the poppy centre.

STAMEN

5. Cut a rectangle from Black crepe paper using OP4 and stretch this strip out to its maximum length. Cut two thin strips of White crepe paper measuring about 1cm (⅜in) wide and the same length as OP4. Stretch these strips and glue them to the same edge on the front and back of your stretched Black strip using white craft glue. Leave to dry.

6. Once dry, cut a few millimetres off the top of the white edge of the strip as this will help trim away any unevenness in the gluing process.

7. Slowly fringe along the entire length of the strip along the white edge – I cut down to about three-quarters of the width.

POPPY CENTRE

8. Attach a 2cm (¾in) foam ball to the tip of a pre-wrapped #18 wire using hot glue. Wrap this foam ball with stretched crepe paper in Light Green.

9. Prepare five small strips of stretched crepe paper in Wine about 3cm (1⅛in) tall and 1cm (⅜in) wide and twist them into noodle-like shapes.

10. Using hot glue, attach the first noodle-like strip across the middle of your wrapped foam ball. Cut the other four noodle shapes in half and glue these smaller strips around the first strip with their ends meeting at the middle, creating a multi-sided star shape for the crown of the poppy head. Be careful when working with hot glue when adding these smaller details. To avoid getting burnt, I usually draw a line of hot glue directly onto my green wrapped centre first, rather than try to put hot glue onto the strip itself.

11. With a thin strip of stretched Light Green crepe paper about 0.5cm (³⁄₁₆in) wide, wrap the sides of the foam ball at its widest portion and hot glue it into place. This helps to hide the uneven ends of each noodle shape and creates a cleaner look to the poppy centre.

12. Glue the fringed stamen around the base of the wrapped foam ball. I tend to ruffle up the fringed stamen at this stage to create a fuzzy texture.

ASSEMBLY

13. Glue three small petals around the stamen as the first layer of petals, followed by the five large petals as the second layer using hot glue.

14. For the calyx, prepare four to five small, rounded triangle shapes from stretched Light Green crepe paper and glue them to the underside of the flowerhead. Wrap the rest of the stalk with stretched Light Green strips to complete the stalk (see *Wrapping*).

1.

2.

3.

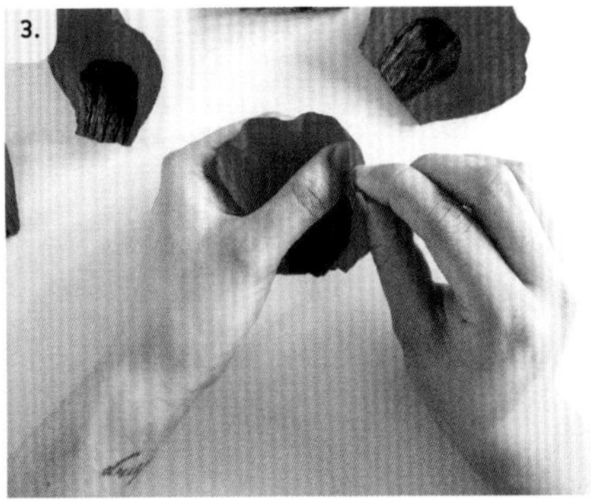

4.

5.

6.

7.

8.

9.

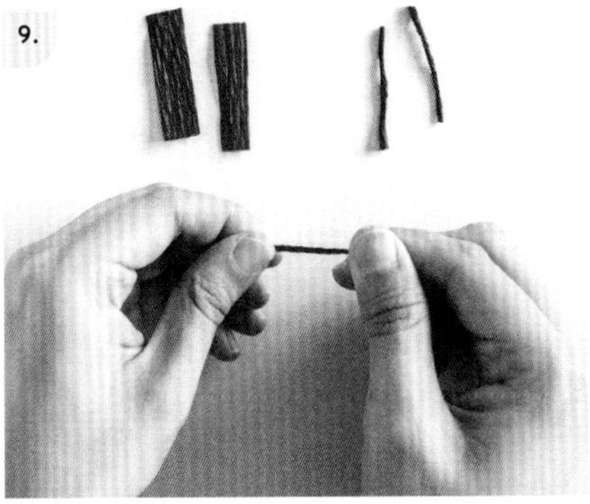

10.

11.

12.

13.

14.

Try other shades of red, yellow or even pink for the crown of the poppy centre to create a contrasting look.

Anemone

DIFFICULTY

Anemones have distinctive black centres that look deceptively simple to make, yet to be frank, it took me a few years to get these centres right! I adore the bicolour anemones for their beautiful red and white juxtaposition, and I've attempted to replicate that design using white acrylic paint. Adding paint is an optional step, however, and you can leave your petals unpainted. While I prefer using stretched crepe, laminated crepe also works if you want thick, hardy petals.

YOU WILL NEED

CREPE PAPER
- Black #602
- Crimson Red #582
- Forest Green #561

OTHER MATERIALS
- Pre-wrapped #18 wire
- 1.5cm (⅝in) foam ball
- White acrylic paint
- Paintbrush
- Wooden skewer
- Scissors and wire cutters
- Mini hot glue gun
- White craft glue

TEMPLATES
Petals: AN1, AN2, AN3
Stamen: AN4
Leaves: AN5

MAIN TECHNIQUES
Cupping, Curling, Fringing, Stretching

FLOWER CENTRE

1. Glue the foam ball to the tip of a pre-wrapped #18 wire with hot glue. Wrap the foam ball with stretched Black crepe paper and hot glue it into place.

2. Cut a strip of Black crepe paper using template AN4 for the stamen. Stretch this strip and fold it in half lengthways.

3. Brush on white acrylic paint to the upper half of the folded Black strip (the folded edge should be the top). The painted layer does not need to be thick or even, as we don't need the stamen to be fully white – just a subtle hint of white paint to distinguish the stamen from the wrapped foam ball.

4. After the white paint has dried, fringe the strip along the folded edge about half of the stamen's width.

5. Wrap the painted stamen around the wrapped foam ball using hot glue.

PETALS

6. From stretched Crimson Red crepe paper, cut three of AN1, four of AN2 and six of AN3. Brush on a light layer of white paint near the base of your petals. This painted layer need not be too thick nor neat, as we will do some touching up at step 15.

7. Gently cup each petal at their bellies for a slight concave once all the paint has dried.

8. Next, with a wooden skewer, gently curl the upper portion of each petal backwards by running the skewer behind the top edges of the petal.

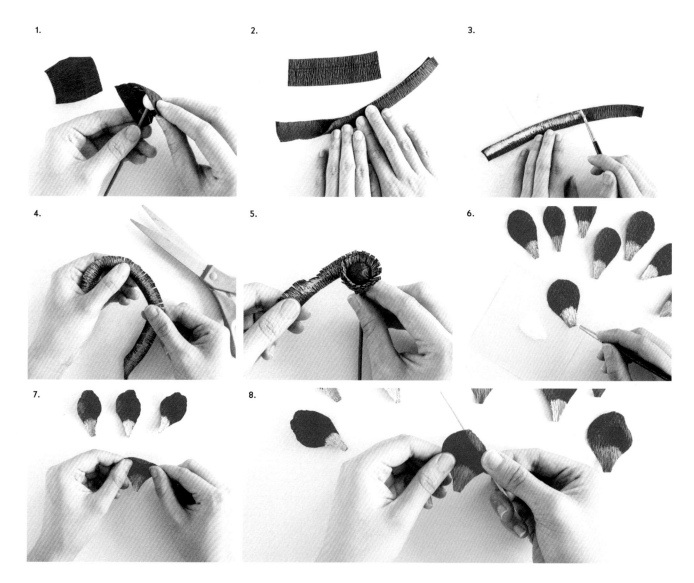

ASSEMBLY

9. Glue on the petals, starting with the three AN1s, with hot glue – use hot glue for all the petals. Anemones are not known for symmetry, so space out the petals in a random fashion.

10. Attach the four AN2 petals next. As much as possible, try not to glue petals directly back-to-back. You want to give each petal room to shine.

11. Finally, glue on the six remaining AN3 petals, using these large petals to fill in any remaining gaps. At this point, it's a good idea to check the top view to ensure that the bloom looks well-balanced.

12. Cut out three leaves from template AN5 in stretched Dark Green. Anemone leaves have a complicated, asymmetrical shape which requires some delicate cutting. If you find them challenging, cut the leaf shape with straight, angular cuts first. Once you have the cut out, you'll find it easier to round the sharp corners one by one.

13. For more lively looking leaves, curl each leaf with a wooden skewer in random directions.

14. I like to glue my leaves right under the flowerhead, but you can glue them lower down the stalk if you prefer.

15. With all the petals assembled, grab your paintbrush again to touch up the white painted layer. The goal is to create a neat white circle around the flower centre.

16. To finish, wrap the rest of the stalk with stretched Dark Green crepe paper strips (see *Wrapping*).

9.

10.

11.

12.

13.

14.

15.

16.

The asymmetrical leaves for anemones are tricky to make and requires some careful cutting. You may find it easier to cut the leaves freehand.

Hydrangea

DIFFICULTY

Hydrangeas are so incredibly gorgeous and there are no other flowers quite like them, yet most paper florists will tell you that they are a pain to make! Be warned, you'll need to cut close to 90 petals for this project. Moreover, in an effort to imitate the lovely lilac and blue hues of actual hydrangeas, I have added an extra step of painting a layer of watercolour. This step might double the time needed but I truly believe the beautiful ombre effect is well worth the extra effort, so please enjoy!

YOU WILL NEED

CREPE PAPER
- Medium Blue #556
- Light Blue #559
- Dark Green #591

OTHER MATERIALS
- Pre-wrapped #18 wire
- #26 wire
- Watercolour paint in blue and purple
- Paintbrush
- Wooden skewer
- Scissors and wire cutters
- Mini hot glue gun
- White craft glue

TEMPLATES
Petals: HY1
Leaves: HY2

MAIN TECHNIQUES
Bow Ties, Cupping, Curling, Laminating

PAINTING

1. Prepare strips of 20cm to 30cm (8in to 12in) long, laminated crepe paper with the same height as template HY1 in a mix of Sky Blue and Light Blue. You need enough strips for about 90 petals. You can choose to have an equal number of strips in both shades of blue, or you can pick a dominant shade of blue and adjust the ratio of strips accordingly.

2. Before painting, have a jar of water and your watercolours (in blue and purple) ready. I like to first brush the top of my laminated strips with a wet paintbrush to prepare the paper. Next, dab on the paint, focusing on just the top half of the strip, alternating between blue and purple.

3. Starting from one end of your laminated strip, make downward strokes with a wet paintbrush, blending the colours downwards and allowing the blues and purples to mix naturally as you work across the strip. Don't worry about the bottom half of your strip as most of this will be trimmed off anyway.

4. The strips will naturally warp and crinkle due to the wet paint, so once the strips are fully dried, stretch them out by pulling on both ends until the strips are flat and even again.

PETALS

5. Cut out as many HY1 petals as you can from each strip by using the accordion fold technique (see *Cutting*). Keep in mind that you will need about 90 petals to create one hydrangea dome.

6. Cup each petal gently, with the painted side facing you.

7. Next, curl each petal away from yourself by running the wooden skewer behind each petal. This combination of cupping and curling may seem contradictory, but it helps to fully stretch out the petals, making them softer in appearance too.

INDIVIDUAL BLOOMS

8. For each small hydrangea bloom, cut a 10cm (4in) piece of #26 wire, and make a fold at the tip. This increases the surface area for us to glue the components on. Wrap each tip with crepe paper in the dominant shade of blue using the bow tie technique.

9. Glue on four petals in a round to complete one hydrangea bloom, remembering to mix the two shades of blue. I tend to use hot glue for this step as it makes the process quicker than using white glue. I usually prefer a 3:1 ratio (so if Sky Blue is the dominant shade, attach three Sky-Blue petals and one Light Blue petal).

10. With white craft glue, wrap the individual bloom stalks below the flowerhead with thin stretched crepe paper strips, using the dominant blue shade (see *Wrapping*).

HYDRANGEA DOME

11. Take 15 blooms and bundle them up into five groups of three, again using stretched crepe paper strips to wrap the bundles together.

12. Select six blooms to form the top of your hydrangea dome. Wrap these six blooms around a pre-wrapped #18 wire, with one bloom right in the centre and five blooms circling that centre bloom.

13. Bend the wired stalks of the bundled trio blooms (from step 11) at a 45-degree angle and wrap them directly below the top six blooms. You want to aim for a rounded dome shape. If you have any extra blooms, use them to fill in any gaps between the bundles.

14. To complete your stalk, make three to six leaves with stretched Dark Green using template HY2. Wrap them along the main stalk using stretched Dark Green to complete your hydrangea (see *Making Leaves* and *Wrapping*).

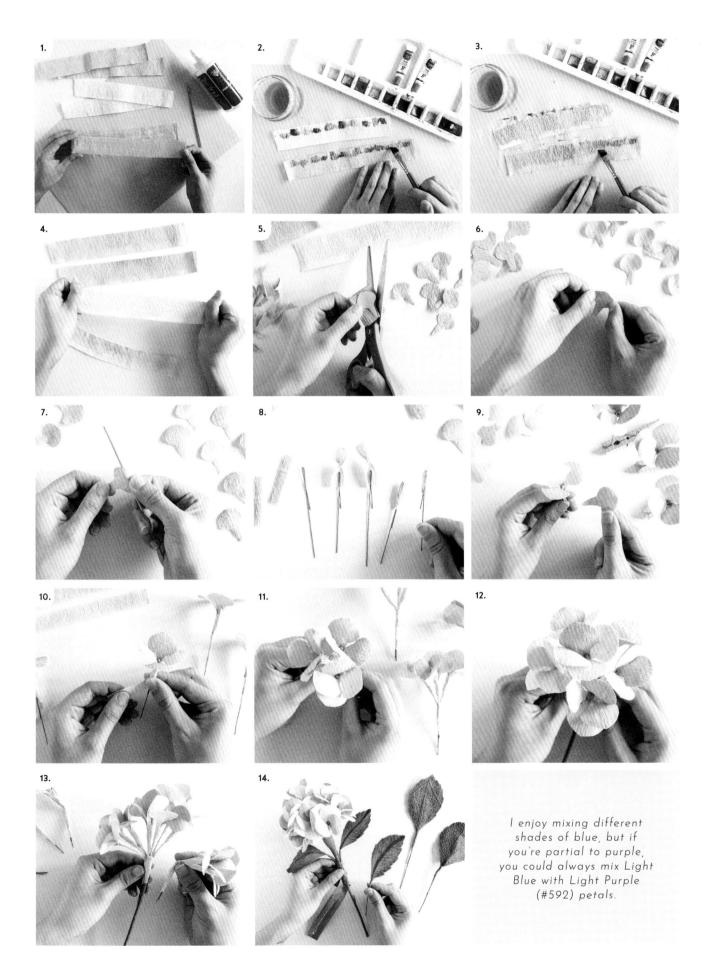

I enjoy mixing different shades of blue, but if you're partial to purple, you could always mix Light Blue with Light Purple (#592) petals.

King Protea

DIFFICULTY

I have always been fascinated by how king proteas can look so strange and almost menacing in appearance, yet they're such popular and sought-after blooms. For a while, I thought it was impossible to recreate this particular bloom in crepe paper, and it took me many attempts to create this version. The project is messy and probably one of the more challenging in this book, so I hope you won't mind getting sticky fingers.

YOU WILL NEED

CREPE PAPER
- Cream #603
- Blush Pink #17A3
- Light Green #562
- Light Brown #567
- Dark Green #591

OTHER MATERIALS
- Pre-wrapped #18 wire
- #24 wire
- Crepe paper scraps
- 8cm (3⅛in) foam disc
- Soft pastels in beige and pink
- Paintbrush
- Scissors and wire cutters
- Mini hot glue gun
- White craft glue

TEMPLATES
Florets: KP1
Bracts: KP2, KP3
Flowerhead: KP4
Leaves: KP5

MAIN TECHNIQUES
Cupping, Fringing

FLORETS

1. Prepare five rectangles using template KP1 in Cream crepe paper. Stretch and fringe each piece about three-quarters of the width.

BRACTS

2. Cut 20 long bracts (KP2), and ten short bracts (KP3) from Blush Pink crepe paper. For some colour detail, rub on soft pastels on both sides of each bract. Rub on a subtle layer of beige at the belly of each bract for a warm tone, followed by a touch of pink right at the tip. Brush to blend.

3. After colouring, gently cup each bract for a gentle concave.

FLOWERHEAD

4. Glue the foam disc onto a short piece of pre-wrapped #18 wire with hot glue. I tend to use a shorter wire first (and extend the stalk only at the end of step 15) since the king protea is very top heavy and we don't want a long stalk to get in our way while we build the flowerhead.

5. Cut two large rectangles from Light Green crepe paper using KP4. Stretch each rectangle piece along the top edge only. You'll notice that as you stretch along the top end, the unstretched base naturally warps and curls inwards, resulting in a rainbow or arch shape.

6. We'll need to build a solid, round dome-shaped base under the foam disc for us to glue on our petals. So, using rolled-up crepe paper scraps, start stuffing and building up a dome-shaped base around the wire. Hold the rolled-up scraps in place with hot glue.

7. Once you have a rough dome shape, grab one piece of KP4 and wrap it over the stuffed dome-shaped base, using hot glue to hold it in place. The longer, stretched end should be at the top, and this end should be long enough to cover the entire circumference of the disc.

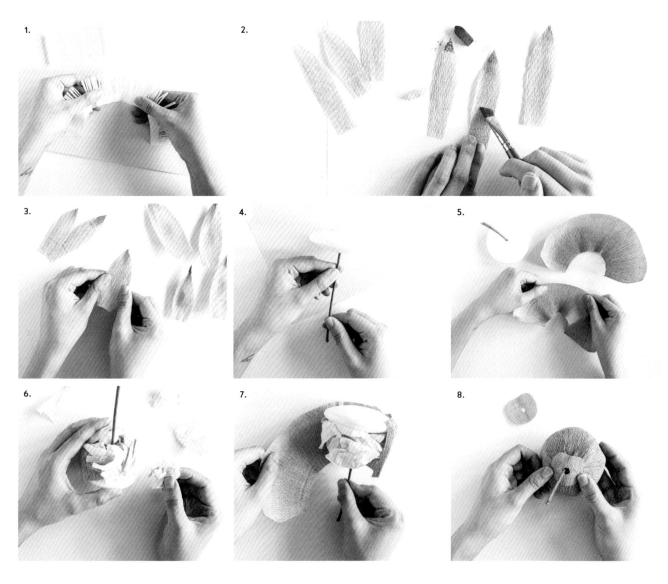

ASSEMBLY

8. To complete the base of the dome, I cut a small donut shape from stretched Light Green crepe paper, poke the wire through it, and glue it down to seal up the stuffed base.

9. We'll now need to create a pointed cone shape for the top of the flowerhead. Do this by gluing on the second piece of stretched KP4 around the top of the disc, with the stretched elongated end attached to the circumference of the disc.

10. Twist at the tip to help define the pointed cone shape and to seal off the peak. You can snip off the pointed tip of the cone if it protrudes out too much.

11. Wrap the fringed pieces of KP1 around the cone tip with hot glue, starting from the peak. Spiral your way downwards until you reach the edge of the foam disc.

12. Once the entire cone is covered, apply a generous amount of white glue to the fringe as a coating.

13. With your fingers, spread the glue over the fringed tips, moulding the tip to seal it off as a small, rounded cone and gluing down the florets as you go. The glue helps to stiffen and harden the florets for a more realistic feel.

14. After the florets have dried, glue on the bracts with hot glue in three layers in this order: ten large bracts (KP2), ten large bracts (KP2) and ten small bracts (KP3). Glue each layer lower than the previous layer so that all three layers cover the entire dome.

15. To thicken and lengthen the stalk, add more pre-wrapped #18 wire to the original stalk, wrapping them together with stretched Light Brown crepe paper strips (see *Wrapping*).

16. Make five to seven leaves (KP5) in stretched Dark Green, using #24 wire, with Light Brown for the petioles (see *Making Leaves*).

9.

10.

11.

12.

13.

16.

14.

15.

Bouquet Ideas

There's something so special about a handmade gift, which is why I wanted to share with you quick and easy bouquet wrapping techniques that will transform your single stalks into sweet gifts for your loved ones. Here's a big tip before you start: don't overthink the wrapping process! Let the folds and creases form naturally in the wrapping paper because overworked paper never looks good.

YOU WILL NEED

- Kraft wrapping paper
- Florist tissue wrapping paper
- Doily
- Twine
- Floral bind wire
- Double-sided tape
- Ribbon

CONE BOUQUET

1a. Start with a rectangular sheet of Kraft wrapping paper, about 21cm by 29cm (8¼in by 11½in). Roll it into a cone shape and secure it with double-sided tape.

1b. Add a doily using the tape and tie a bow around it with the twine.

1c. Wrap a piece of florist tissue wrapping paper around the base of your bloom and secure it with floral bind wire. Push the wrapped end into the cone, it should fit snugly!

GIFT BOUQUET

2a. Cut your wrapping paper into squares. Position the first piece in a diamond shape behind your bloom. Pinch in and bunch up the paper tightly around the stalk below the leaves.

2b. Repeat for the next sheet, positioning it slightly off to the side.

2c. Add as many sheets as you like and complete with a matching ribbon.

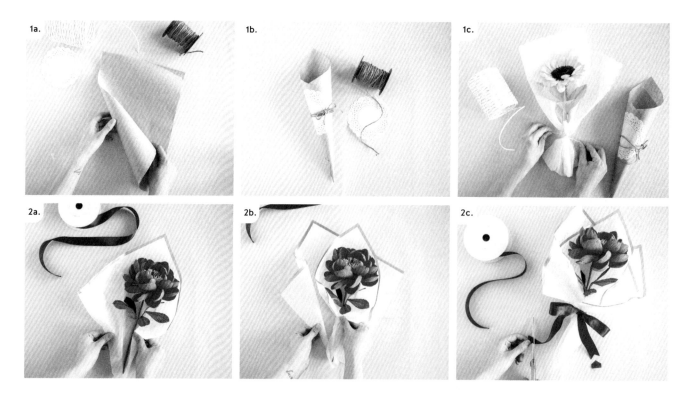

Bugs and Butterflies

Butterflies

DIFFICULTY

One of my biggest goals for this book is to offer handmade bugs that are easy to make and not wildly intimidating, because crafting should never be scary! Here we have two distinct butterflies to demonstrate a couple of straightforward approaches to butterfly making. We will make both bodies, then focus on the wing pattern for the Monarch butterfly and the wing venation for the Blue Morpho before assembling the pieces for both species. Once you are comfortable with the two different wing techniques, you can combine them to make all kinds of wonderful butterflies!

YOU WILL NEED

CREPE PAPER
Body:
- Black #602
- White #600

Monarch wings:
- Black #602
- Orange #610

Blue Morpho wings:
- Medium Blue #556

OTHER MATERIALS
- #24 and #26 wire
- Soft pastels in orange, yellow, light blue, dark blue and aquamarine
- White acrylic paint
- Fine-tipped paintbrush
- Black permanent marker
- Wooden skewer
- Bone folder
- Long-nose pliers
- Scissors and wire cutters
- Mini hot glue gun
- White craft glue

TEMPLATES
Body: BUG1

Monarch wings: MB1, MB2, MB3, MB4

Blue Morpho wings: BMB1, BMB2

MAIN TECHNIQUES
Fringing, Laminating, Stretching, Wrapping

BODIES AND FEELERS

1. With the help of the long-nose pliers, bend a piece of #26 wire multiple times backwards and forwards in a zigzag to make each butterfly body. The finished body for the Monarch needs to be about 6cm (2¼in) to accommodate the larger wings and for the Blue Morpho about 5cm (2in) long.

2. For the feelers, cut two 6cm (2¼in) pieces of #26 wire for each butterfly. Wrap them with thin strips of stretched Black crepe paper, giving added emphasis to the tips. Once the feelers are done, wrap them in pairs with a body, using more stretched Black crepe paper.

3. Continue to wrap the entire length of each butterfly body in stretched Black crepe paper. I like to wrap extra layers around the upper halves to suggest a head.

4. Use template BUG1 to cut small rectangles from Black crepe paper. Stretch each rectangle, fold in half lengthways and fringe along the unfolded side. Snip these fringed strips into shorter 1cm (⅜in) or 2cm (¾in) strips. Repeat to make a few White stretched crepe paper pieces for the Monarch. We will use these fringed pieces to add texture to the butterfly bodies.

5. Starting from the bottom and with the fringes pointing downwards, hot glue the pieces across the bodies to create layers. Space the strips further apart along the lower half and closer together on the upper half of each body, again to emphasise the head. Include some fringed strips of white across the top half of the slightly longer Monarch body for extra detail.

1.

2.

3.

4.

5.

WINGS: MONARCH

6. Prepare laminated Black crepe paper, then cut two each of wing templates MB1 and MB2. From stretched Orange crepe paper, cut two each of wing templates MB3 and MB4, plus two extra ovals.

7. Add soft pastels in orange and yellow to the Orange shapes to create an ombre effect. Blend with a paintbrush.

8. Glue an Orange MB3 piece and a small oval to each Black top wing, then glue an Orange MB4 piece to each Black bottom wing. Draw in the line details in black permanent marker, as shown, shading rounded edges for the Orange segments.

9. Using the paintbrush, add small dots of white acrylic paint along the edges of the wings.

10. Once the paint has dried, we will coat each wing with a layer of white craft glue. First apply it around the edges of the wing and make checkered lines across the centre. Next, spread out the glue in an even layer using a wooden skewer, ensuring that you cover the complete surface. This coat of white glue helps to seal in the colours and adds a glossy shine to the wings. Leave to dry as you make the wings for the Blue Morpho butterfly.

6.

7.

8.

9.

10.

If freehand drawing makes you nervous, use a pencil to trace the designs first. Place the wings side by side to add the details, mirroring the pattern on the first set.

WINGS: BLUE MORPHO

11. Cut out four each of templates BMB1 and BMB2 from stretched Medium Blue crepe paper. For each wing, we will require two layers – a top layer and a base layer.

12. To create the wing veins, prepare some short pieces of #26 wire – you will need five or six pieces per wing. Use white craft glue to draw the vein pattern in thin lines onto the four base wings layer (you may prefer to draw the pattern out in pencil first – see Tip on previous page), then you are ready to stick on the wires one by one. Bend them gently into shape and press into place.

13. Each wing needs a top layer and a base layer for the lamination. Spread a thin layer of white glue over the four top wings – in a similar way to our usual lamination technique – and glue each one over the corresponding base layer.

14. Press down firmly to ensure the vein pattern is defined and protruding. Use a bone folder or the rounded end of a brush to work around the pattern, emphasising the veins.

15. Rub on soft pastels in light and dark blues to create an ombre effect on the wings. Brush to blend. I sometimes like to add a hint of aquamarine as well.

16. Colour in the edges of the wings with a black permanent marker. Colour in a scalloped edge following the vein pattern.

17. Add a few white spots along the edges of the wings using white acrylic paint and a fine paintbrush.

18. For a glossy finish and to seal in the colours, coat each wing with a generous layer of white glue as you did for the Monarch butterfly in step 10. Leave to dry completely before you move on to assemble both butterflies.

ASSEMBLING THE BUTTERFLIES

19. Starting with the slightly longer Monarch, prepare a small rectangle of stretched Black crepe paper for the backing. Trim the corners so that they are slightly curved for a cleaner look. Cut two short pieces of #24 wire and glue them as two parallel lines across the backing rectangle. This wired backing provides extra support, helps to hold everything together and also allows you to pose the wings.

20. Using hot glue, stick the wings to the Black backing, starting with the lower pair and leaving a narrow gap in between the left and right wings. Add the upper pair, maintaining the gap in the middle.

21. Apply a generous amount of hot glue directly into the narrow gap and quickly attach the body. Once secure, adjust the wings by bending them inwards or outwards to your liking. You can also gently cup the wings at this point to give them a slight curve.

22. For the Blue Morpho, cut the backing rectangle from Medium Blue crepe paper to match the wings. Add the two parallel wires, then attach the wings as you did for the Monarch in step 20.

23. As the wings are already wired, you can cup and curve them before finally adding the body in between with hot glue.

Bees

DIFFICULTY

I was once stung by a bee, and while that painful experience makes me a tad fearful of the real thing, I am absolutely smitten by these crepe paper versions. With round chubby bodies and tiny wings, these adorable bees are guaranteed not to sting! I love placing them around my studio using a magnet backing, but they would also look super cute suspended in mini glass domes. In case you prefer not to use foam, you can substitute the foam balls with scrunched up crepe paper scraps.

YOU WILL NEED

CREPE PAPER

- White #600
- Yellow #576
- Lemon Yellow #575
- Black #602

OTHER MATERIALS

- #24 and #26 wire
- 1.5cm (⅝in) and 2cm (¾in) foam balls or crepe paper scraps
- Black permanent marker
- Long-nose pliers
- Penknife
- Scissors and wire cutters
- Mini hot glue gun
- White craft glue

TEMPLATES

Body: BUG1
Wings: BEE1, BEE2

MAIN TECHNIQUES

Fringing, Stretching, Wrapping

BODY

1. For the bee's head, slice a small 1.5cm (⅝in) foam ball in half with a penknife. Join the head to a 2cm (¾in) foam ball body by poking a short #24 wire through both, then add glue and push together to secure.

2. Wrap around the join with a small piece of stretched White crepe paper. This will make it easier for us to wrap subsequent layers.

3. Using BUG1, cut rectangular strips of White, Yellow, Lemon Yellow and Black crepe paper. Stretch each strip lengthways, fold in half, and fringe along the unfolded end.

4. Starting from the bottom, and with the fringes pointing downwards, wrap the fringed strips around the bee's body. Work your way upwards, alternating the colours as you wish.

5. Wrap all the way up to the tip of the head, leaving a small gap at the top for the feelers.

FEELERS AND LEGS

6. For each of the two feelers and six legs, cut 3cm (1⅛in) pieces of wire (use #26 for the feelers and #24 for the legs) and wrap them with thin strips of stretched Black crepe paper. For the legs, I like to wrap them thicker in the middle. With pliers, bend the legs to create sharp 'Z' shapes.

7. Dab the ends of the feelers with white craft glue and poke them into the tip of the bee's head (see Tip).

8. To cover the space between the feelers, take small fringed pieces of Black crepe paper and glue them into the gap. You can also add extra fringed strips around the feelers if needed.

9. Once the head is completely covered, poke the legs into the sides of the body. I prefer to poke in all six legs without glue first, which allows me to make adjustments and check that they look somewhat symmetrical before committing to gluing them.

WINGS

10. Stretch some White crepe paper and cut two upper wings using BEE1, then two lower wings using BEE2. Trace out the line detail from the template using a black permanent marker.

11. For a glossy effect, coat each wing with a thin layer of white glue and leave to dry.

12. Apply a spot of hot glue on the narrowest end of each wing and glue them directly onto the sides of the body, right above the legs.

1.

2.

3.

4.

5.

6.

7.

When adding the feelers and legs, you may find it helpful to use a pin or a needle to poke the holes into the foam ball head and body first.

8.

9.

10.

11.

12.

Beetles

DIFFICULTY

Here are the most colourful and cheerful beetles you will ever see! If you have been collecting leftover crepe paper scraps, this is a great project to put them to good use. There's only one template and no rules for these not-so-creepy-crawlies, so feel free to mix all sorts of colours and patterns to create your very own quirky, one-of-a-kind beetle. These look great in a frame, or you can attach a magnet backing and pop it on your refrigerator, easy as pie!

YOU WILL NEED

YOU WILL NEED

CREPE PAPER

- Black #602
- Lilac #592
- Medium Purple #590
- Dark Purple #593

OTHER MATERIALS

- #22 and #26 wire
- Crepe paper scraps
- Needle
- Long-nose pliers
- Scissors and wire cutters
- Mini hot glue gun
- White craft glue

TEMPLATES

Head: Bug1

MAIN TECHNIQUES

Bow Ties, Fringing

BODY AND HEAD

1. Scrunch up crepe paper scraps in any colour into three round shapes in three sizes: the largest for the beetle's abdomen, medium for the thorax and the smallest for the head. Roll them up in between your palms and mould them with your fingers to achieve the desired shapes.

2. Using the bow tie technique, wrap each body part with the crepe paper colour of your choice and glue them down with hot glue. I tend to pick two similar colour shades and alternate them across the three body parts.

3. For the head, cut strips of crepe paper in two colours using template Bug1. Stretch, fold and fringe each strip, similar to what we do for the bees and butterflies. Snip these into smaller fringed pieces and wrap around the front of the head with the fringe pointing downwards, alternating colours for each layer. Hold them in place with hot glue.

4. For the eyes, roll two tiny balls from stretched Black crepe paper, you can use scraps for this too! Glue them onto the head with hot glue. For the feelers, prepare two pieces of #26 wire about 5cm (2in) long. Wrap them using thin, stretched crepe paper strips – I sometimes wrap the tips of the feelers in a different colour for a fun detail. Poke the feelers through the head using a needle to create small holes first.

If you want to make a shorter beetle, you can exclude the thorax, or medium shape, from step 1.

WINGS

5. Cut two rectangles from crepe paper for the wings. Make sure they are longer than your beetle's abdomen. Trim away the four corners to round the edges.

6. With hot glue, attach the two wings to the top of the abdomen, gently shaping them to follow the curve of the body. Trim the ends of the wings at this point to ensure that both sides are even.

7. Glue on round shapes cut from different colours of crepe paper to create your own wing pattern. I prefer to use hot glue for this step, but you can use white craft glue if the shapes are very small.

LEGS

8. Prepare six pieces of #22 wire about 5cm (2in) long and wrap them in your chosen colour. To differentiate the leg segments, add cuffs or bands near the tip and at the base of each leg using tiny pieces of unstretched crepe paper in a contrasting colour and wrapping them around the wrapped wire with hot glue. After adding the bands, bend each segment to form a 'Z' shape with pliers.

ASSEMBLY

9. Glue the head, thorax and abdomen together with a generous amount of hot glue. Position the legs so that there is one leg on each side of the thorax and two legs on each side of the abdomen.

10. Use a needle to help with poking the initial holes before attaching the legs. Secure each leg with hot glue and adjust the legs so that they sit nicely to the sides when the beetle is flat on the ground.

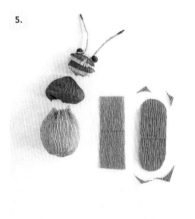

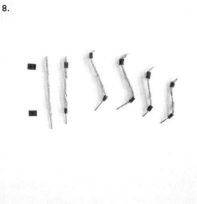

Io Moths

DIFFICULTY

This Io Moth was a late addition to the book, mainly because I wanted to include a small, cute and cuddly moth to contrast with the large, regal Atlas Moth. I have to admit, the furry wings were a huge challenge! As the wings are already small to begin with, creating the fine fur details calls for some precise cutting and gluing skills. Nonetheless, the extra fuzz is my favourite part and I think it truly makes a difference in bringing the Io Moth's personality to life.

YOU WILL NEED

CREPE PAPER
- Orange #610
- Yellow #576
- Rouge Pink #547

OTHER MATERIALS
- Pre-wrapped #18 wire
- #26 wire
- 1.5cm (⅝in) foam ball
- Soft pastels in pink, orange and blue
- White acrylic paint
- Fine-tipped paintbrush
- Black and maroon permanent markers
- Needle
- Wooden skewer
- Scissors and wire cutters
- Mini hot glue gun
- White craft glue

TEMPLATES
Body: Bug2
Wings: IO1, IO2

MAIN TECHNIQUES
Fringing, Laminating, Wrapping

FEELERS

1. Cut two small teardrop shapes from stretched crepe paper in Orange, about 2cm (¾in) tall. Glue on a 3cm (1⅛in) piece of #26 wire wrapped in Orange along the middle of each teardrop shape. Fringe along both sides, making diagonal cuts to mimic the moth's feelers.

BODY

2. Hot glue the small foam ball onto the tip of a 3cm (1⅛in) piece of pre-wrapped #18 wire. Wrap the entire length of the body with stretched Yellow crepe paper, using either hot glue or white glue.

3. Using template Bug2, cut the following rectangular strips: six Yellow, one Orange and one Rouge Pink, with each strip about 10cm (4in) long. Stretch each strip, fold in half, and fringe along the unfolded edge. To wrap the body, cut a few Yellow fringed strips into shorter strips of between 2cm to 3cm (¾in to 1⅛in) long. For the furry texture later, cut several Yellow, Orange and Rouge Pink fringed strips into much smaller 0.5cm (³⁄₁₆in) strips and set them aside for step 10.

4. Working from the bottom of the body upwards, start wrapping the body with the Yellow fringed strips layer by layer with the fringe pointing downwards, similar to a piñata. Use hot glue to attach the fringed strips.

5. Once you've reached the head, poke two holes with a needle and attach the two feelers right at the top. Add hot glue to hold them in place.

WINGS

6. Prepare laminated Yellow crepe paper, then cut two each of the upper and lower wings (IO1 and IO2) . Since these wings are small, we don't need to use wire to reinforce them.

7. With a maroon marker, draw in the leopard print design on the upper wings, plus a scalloped border nearer to the wing's outer edge. Add a thick maroon border to the lower wings. For an ombre effect, I shade in a layer of pinkish-orange with soft pastels to the inner corners of each wing and blend outwards with a paintbrush. Your designs need not be perfect but try to aim for symmetry across the left and right wings.

8. For the lower wings, draw a circle using black permanent marker. Shade the inside of the circle with a soft pastel in blue, then brush gently within the circle to blend.

9. With white acrylic paint, dab on a few spots to highlight the black circle. You can use a fine-tipped paintbrush or the end of a wooden skewer. Once the paint has dried, you can glue the upper and lower wings together by gluing the edges and slightly overlapping the wings.

10. Now we can start adding the furry bits! Scrunch up the short-fringed pieces from step 3 by twisting or pinching their folded ends. This should make the fringed portion fan out.

11. Glue the individual fringed pieces one by one to the inner corners of the wings to build up a fluffy texture. I use hot glue to hold them in place so that I can work quickly. You can add as many or as few of these fringed pieces as you want.

12. Create an ombre effect across the upper and lower wings with three colours. Start by building up a base of Rouge Pink fuzz on the lower wing, transition to Orange in the middle (where the wings intersect), and end with Yellow fringe right at the top. You can fluff up the fringe with your fingers to enhance the fuzzy texture. Make sure the left and right wings have the same pattern.

ASSEMBLY

13. Glue all the wings to a strip of stretched Yellow crepe paper with a generous amount of hot glue (this strip serves as a backing).

14. Finally, attach the body to the same backing with hot glue and bend the wings so that the fuzz from the wings blend in seamlessly with the fur on the body.

Atlas Moths

DIFFICULTY

This moth was one of the first crepe paper bugs I ever made, and I still find it challenging even now! As we rely heavily on colouring with soft pastels, markers and paint, I would suggest practising on the Monarch butterfly or the Io Moth first before tackling this large moth. While my Atlas Moth's body is by no means anatomically accurate, I do love how chubby and colourful it looks, and you can have fun by changing up the colours for each layer as well.

YOU WILL NEED

CREPE PAPER

- Orange #610
- Dark Brown #568
- Rouge Pink #547
- Wine #588

OTHER MATERIALS

- Pre-wrapped #18 wire
- #24 and #26 wire
- 1.5cm (⅝in) foam ball
- Soft pastels in pink or red
- White acrylic paint
- Fine-tipped paintbrush
- Black, brown and maroon permanent markers
- Needle
- Scissors and wire cutters
- Mini hot glue gun
- White craft glue

TEMPLATES

Body: Bug2
Wings:
- AM1 (top base wings)
- AM2 (bottom base wings)
- AM3, AM4 (wing pattern)

MAIN TECHNIQUES

Fringing, Laminating

FEELERS

1. Prepare two 4cm (1⅝in) lengths of #26 wire for the feelers and wrap them with thin strips of Orange crepe paper. Cut a small teardrop shape about 3cm (1⅛in) long from stretched Orange crepe paper for each feeler. With white craft glue, attach one wrapped wire along the middle of the teardrop shape. Fringe along both sides, making diagonal cuts, to make each feeler.

BODY

2. As the body of the Atlas Moth is wider at the base, I glue one small foam ball at the bottom of a 4cm (1⅝in) piece of pre-wrapped #18 wire, as opposed to the top. Wrap the entire length of the body with stretched Dark Brown crepe paper to give the body more volume. I also wrap additional layers at the top to round out the head. I use hot glue for this step but you could use white craft glue.

3. To create a fluffy texture to the body, add fringed strips using template Bug2. I'm using Dark Brown, Orange, Rouge Pink and Wine. Stretch each strip, fold in half, and fringe along the unfolded edge. Snip these fringed strips into shorter strips of 2cm to 3cm (¾in to 1⅛in) long to wrap around the body.

4. Starting from the bottom of the body and working upwards, wrap the body with the fringed strips in alternating layers, like a piñata, gluing them down with hot glue. Make sure the fringe points downwards. I like to create a brown and yellow striped pattern on the wider bottom and use the pinks to distinguish the head.

5. Once the body is complete, attach the two feelers to the top of the moth body and secure them in place with a dab of hot glue. You can use a needle to poke the initial holes first before gluing them on.

WINGS

6. Cut out four AM1s and four AM2s from stretched Dark Brown crepe paper. As these wings are large, we'll want to laminate the wings and reinforce them with wire in between the laminated layers. To do so, glue on short pieces of #26 wire right along the top edges of AM1 and the bottom edges of AM2 before laminating them with the top wing layer using white craft glue.

7. Cut two each of AM3 and AM4 from stretched Orange crepe paper. Apply a thin layer of white glue to each shape and glue them on top of each brown wing (AM3 goes onto AM1 and AM4 onto AM2). With a maroon marker, shade in the outline of the orange shapes, and draw in the scalloped lines and dot patterns as shown. Add shading under the scalloped lines.

8. Next, rub on soft pastels in pinkish-orange or pinkish-red for an ombre effect. I usually shade along the orange edge above the dot pattern, as well as right below the scalloped lines. Blend with a brush.

9. When you're happy with the blend of colours, go back with a darker brown marker to emphasise the scalloped and dotted details.

10. We can now paint in the white details. Use a fine paintbrush to paint on white lines and rounded triangular shapes on the wings. While you don't need to be very neat and precise with your wing designs, I do recommend aiming for symmetry across the left and right wings.

11. After the paint has dried, add in some rough outlines around the white designs with a black marker.

ASSEMBLY

12. Cut a small piece of stretched Dark Brown crepe paper and glue on two to three short pieces of #24 wire with hot glue. This will serve as the backing for our moth.

13. Glue on the four wings with a gap in between the right and left wings, again using hot glue.

14. With a generous amount of hot glue, attach the moth body to the backing. Bend the wings around the body and adjust them to your liking.

1.

2.

3.

4.

5.

6.

7.

8.

9.

10.

11.

12.

13.

14.

ATLAS MOTHS

Dragonflies

DIFFICULTY

No crepe paper bug collection is complete without these playful, googly-eyed dragonflies. I've intentionally made each dragonfly dichromatic so that it is easy to match colours. I recommend choosing crepe paper shades in the same colour family (for example dark blue and light blue) and to always pick the darker shade for the wings. You can add legs to them if you like, however, I find it easier to stick them on walls or vases with flat backs.

YOU WILL NEED

CREPE PAPER
- Medium Blue #556
- Dark Blue #555

OTHER MATERIALS
- #26 wire
- Crepe paper scraps in White
- Soft pastels in white
- Paintbrush
- Bone folder
- Long-nose pliers
- Scissors and wire cutters
- Mini hot glue gun
- White craft glue

TEMPLATES
Head: Bug1
Wings: DF1

MAIN TECHNIQUES
Fringing, Laminating, Wrapping

BODY

1. With some pliers, bend a piece of #26 wire backwards and forwards in a zigzag to create a body that's 10cm (4in) long.

2. With stretched Medium Blue crepe paper strips and white craft glue, wrap the entire length of the body to create bulk. I usually use multiple strips to achieve the ideal thickness: the lower 6cm (2¼in) of the body should be around 4mm (⁵⁄₃₂in) wide, while the head (upper 4cm or 1⅝in of the body) should be about 1cm (⅜in) wide.

3. To add texture to the body, prepare small strips of crepe paper (Bug1) in both colours, then stretch, fold and fringe each strip. Snip into smaller fringed pieces and wrap across the body with the fringe pointing downwards, gluing each piece down with hot glue. Start from the base of the body and work your way upwards strip by strip. To create a pattern, I like to alternate colours near the tail and head of the dragonfly.

4. For the eyes, roll two small balls from Dark Blue crepe paper. Prepare two even smaller rolled-up balls in White for the centres. I tend to use crepe paper scraps for the eyes. Hot glue them to the top of the dragonfly head.

WINGS

5. As we'll need to laminate the wings with wire to create veins, cut eight wings (DF1) from stretched Dark Blue crepe paper. On four of the wings, draw out the wing veins with white craft glue and stick on 7cm (2¾in) pieces of #26 wire, bending them slightly to mimic the wing pattern. You can use the wing design on the template to guide you. This is same technique as making the wings for the Blue Morpho butterfly.

6. Once the wire is glued on, laminate each wing with a corresponding top layer of DF1.

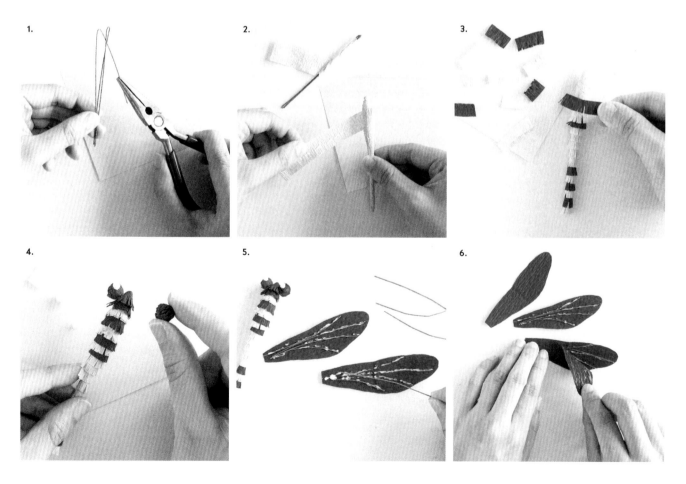

ASSEMBLY

7. Press down firmly on the top layer so that the wing veins are clearly defined. With a bone folder or the end of a paintbrush, carve along the wired design to emphasise the veins.

8. To further accentuate the wings, I like to brush on a layer of white soft pastel, but only to the bottom half of each wing to help create a pretty ombre effect.

9. Remember to make four wings in total, two wings for each side of the dragonfly.

10. To make the backing of your dragonfly, prepare a small rectangular strip of stretched crepe paper with rounded corners in a matching shade.

11. Glue the four wings onto this backing with hot glue. I usually don't overlap the top and bottom dragonfly wings as they're quite narrow. Leave a narrow gap in between the left and right wings for the body.

12. With the wings all done, glue on the body using a generous amount of hot glue. Bend and position the wings to your liking.

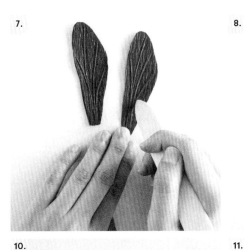

Display Ideas

I had never known it was possible to craft insects from crepe paper until I saw the gorgeous moths and butterflies made by Kathryn Bondy (@goldenagebotanicals). Her lifelike pieces were the main inspiration behind my own exploration into the world of not-so-creepy crawlies. I knew I wanted to put my own colourful spin on bugs to make them as vibrant and whimsical as I could! Once you've made these friendly bugs, you are probably wondering how to display them. These bugs are generally light enough to be stuck on the wall with Blu Tac, but here are three other great ways to showcase your handmade creations.

MAGNETS

1. Small round magnets are perfect for attaching to the back of your crepe paper bugs. Hot glue might not work on the magnet's surface, so I usually make a tight pocket using a thick strip of stretched crepe paper. This pocket allows me to slot the flat magnet snugly inside. Once the magnet is attached, you're free to stick your bug to your fridge and metal cabinets!

FRAMES AND PLAQUES

2. Deep shadowbox frames are great for displaying bugs, and you can add scrapbooking or patterned paper as the background. Alternatively, you can opt for wooden plaques that come in a variety of fun shapes and designs. A nice coat of paint can help your bug truly stand out.

GLASS DOMES

3. Lastly, glass domes are fun ways to show off your bugs. If your glass dome comes with a wooden base, you can drill a small hole and suspend your bug using florist wire. You could also create a diorama by gluing on branches to the base in order to prop up your bug.

For glass domes without a wooden base, you'll have to get more creative, and I usually rely simply on friction. For instance, you can stack multiple beetles together in a small dome – the friction between the beetles' legs and the glass casing should be enough to keep everything in place!

Potted Plants

POTTED PLANTS

Daffodils and Irises

DIFFICULTY

Mark the arrival of spring by crafting your own little garden of daffodils and irises! I've paired them up for this tutorial as they are both petite flowers that are easy to make and they both have similar leaf designs. I love how the two blooms look together in a pot. The contrasting heights neatly separates the dwarf irises from the tall crowns of the sunny daffodils, creating a beautiful arrangement with bright, eye-catching colours, radiating nothing but warmth and cheerfulness.

YOU WILL NEED

Daffodil:
- Orange #610
- Vanilla #577

Iris:
- Dark Purple #593
- White #600
- Yellow #576

Leaves:
- Dark Green #591
- Forest Green #561

OTHER MATERIALS
- Pre-wrapped #18 wire
- Wooden skewer
- Scissors and wire cutters
- Mini hot glue gun
- White craft glue

TEMPLATES

Daffodil corona: DAF1

Daffodil petal: DAF2

Iris petals: IR1, IR2, IR3

Iris petal detail: IR4, IR5

MAIN TECHNIQUES

Bow Ties, Cupping, Curling, Fluting, Laminating

DAFFODIL CORONA AND PETALS

1. For the daffodil corona, cut a large rectangle from Orange crepe paper using DAF1. Draw a thin line of white glue along one of the shorter edges.

2. Create a cylinder by looping the rectangle around itself and stick the opposite end onto the glued margin, creating a slight overlap. Leave to dry (you can use wooden pegs to hold the glued portion in place while the glue is drying).

3. After the glue has dried, gently curl back the tips of the corona with a wooden skewer.

4. Prepare laminated Vanilla crepe paper for the petals and cut six of DAF2. Cup each petal at their bellies and curl the tips backwards with a wooden skewer.

DAFFODIL CENTRE AND ASSEMBLY

5. For the three daffodil stamen, simply twist narrow strips of Vanilla crepe paper, about 5.5cm (2⅜in) long, into noodle-like shapes. Leave the tip untwisted so there's a tiny triangular shape right at the top.

6. Prepare your stalk by covering the tip of a pre-wrapped #18 wire with Vanilla crepe paper (see *Bow Ties*). Wrap the three stamen around the tip of the wire with matching stretched crepe paper strips.

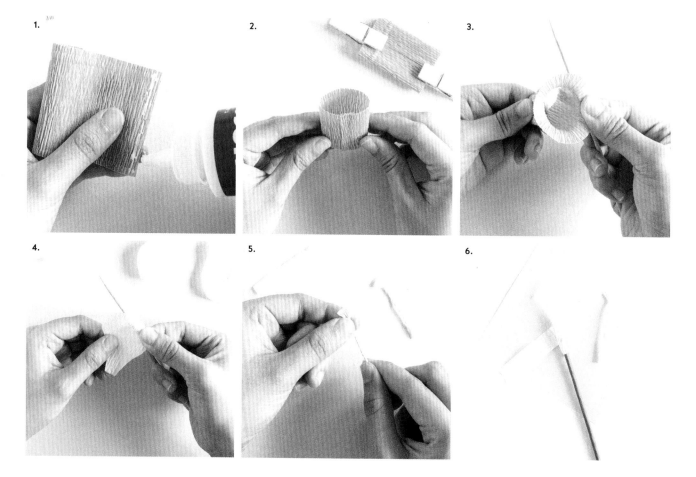

1.

2.

3.

4.

5.

6.

7. Next, insert the stalk through the corona and pinch the bottom end of the corona around your wire. With a thin, stretched crepe paper strip in Vanilla and some white glue, wrap the bottom end of the corona onto the wire, making sure it is wrapped tightly.

8. Push down into the base of the corona with your fingers to round out the bottom. The resulting shape should look something like a 'U' or an inverted bell.

9. I also like to crinkle the curled-back tip of the corona by pinching the edges to create creases (similar to the fluting technique in *Making Leaves*).

10. Once you're satisfied with the look of the corona, glue on the first three petals in a triangle formation around the base of corona. I use hot glue to attach all my petals quickly.

11. Glue the next three petals in the gaps between the first three petals. For added texture, pinch the tips and give them a good tug outwards after they are all glued on. This naturally prompts a crease to form through the centre of the petal.

7.

8.

9.

10.

11.

IRIS PETALS

12. Prepare laminated crepe paper in Dark Purple and cut three IR1s, three IR2s and six IR3s.

13. For each petal, gently cup them at their widest point.

14. For the detail at the centre of the petal, cut three of IR4 in stretched Yellow and three of IR5 in stretched White crepe paper.

15. Carefully cut out triangles to form spikes along the top border of all the IR5s.

16. Attach one IR5, followed by one IR4 to each large iris (IR1) petal using white craft glue.

17. Next, with hot glue, attach two IR3s to the base of each large IR1 petal. Glue them side by side.

IRIS ASSEMBLY

18. Wrap the tip of a short piece of pre-wrapped #18 wire with Dark Purple crepe paper, using the bow tie technique. Start assembling the iris bloom by first attaching three IR2s in a layer around the wrapped wire tip.

19. Glue on the three IR1 petals in between the IR2s.

20. Gently press down the large petals so that they curl downwards.

DAFFODILS AND IRIS LEAVES

21. As the leaves for daffodils and irises tend to be narrow, hardy and tall, I like to use unstretched crepe paper. First, cut out thin strips from Dark Green or Forest Green crepe paper, with each strip measuring about 1.5cm to 2cm (⅝in to ¾in) wide. You can vary the heights according to the height of your flower stalk, and pair whichever colour you like with the flowers.

22. Trim the tips of each narrow strip to create a pointed edge. Gently cup the leaf as well, especially the lower half of the leaf, to expand its surface area.

23. After cupping, fold the leaves in half lengthways, as this creates a sharper, more rigid look to the leaves.

24. After wrapping the stalks in stretched crepe paper to match the leaves (see *Wrapping*), glue on the leaves near the base of the stalk with hot glue.

12.

13.

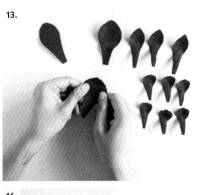

14.

15.

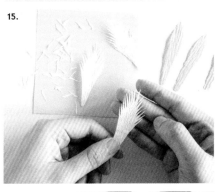

16.

17.

18.

To make a larger iris, simply enlarge the template sizes of the petals according to how big you want your bloom.

19.

20.

21.

22.

23.

24.

POTTED PLANTS

Orchids

DIFFICULTY

For me, orchids have been one of the more challenging flowers to recreate. I struggled for a long time with the orchid centres before finally deciding to worry less about botanical accuracy and focus more on having fun! That's why the orchid centres you see here are playful, whimsical and, most importantly, easy to make. A side note – although the three petal-like components behind the two frontal petals are scientifically classified as sepals, I have called them petals here for simplicity's sake.

YOU WILL NEED

CREPE PAPER
- Magenta #572
- Blush Pink #17A3
- Forest Green #561

OTHER MATERIALS
- Pre-wrapped #18 wire
- #22 and #26 wire
- 3 x 1.5cm (⅝in) foam balls
- Soft pastels in pinks, yellows and browns
- Paintbrush
- Fine-tipped brush marker in dark pink or maroon
- Wooden skewer
- Long-nose pliers
- Scissors and wire cutters
- Mini hot glue gun
- White craft glue

TEMPLATES
Petals: O1, O2, O3, O4
Leaves: O5

MAIN TECHNIQUES
Bow Ties, Cupping, Curling, Laminating, Wrapping

PETALS

1. Prepare laminated crepe paper in Magenta and Blush Pink. For each individual orchid bloom, cut two of template O1 and three of O2 in Magenta, and one O3 and one O4 in Blush Pink.

2. Gently cup petals O1 and O2 at their widest point. With a wooden skewer, gently curl the top left and right edges of each petal backwards.

3. For the O3 petal, cup the two rounded sides. For the O4 petal, cup near the base. After both components are cupped, attach O3 to the middle of O4 with white craft glue to form the orchid centre. Leave to dry.

4. Using soft pastels, colour in the orchid centre with pinks and yellows. Brush to blend.

5. Add a drop of hot glue to the middle of O3 and pinch from behind – this helps to add a 3D structure to the orchid centre.

6. To further shape the orchid centre, pinch the two sides of O3 and curl the bottom of O4 with a wooden skewer. All your petals are now ready to assemble.

FLOWER ASSEMBLY

7. Bend a piece of #26 wire in half and wrap the folded tip with Magenta crepe paper using the bow tie technique.

8. Apply hot glue to the tip of O4 and attach it to the wrapped tip. Next, glue two O1s to the sides, followed by the three O2s in a triangular formation behind the two large frontal petals.

9. Wrap the flower stalk beneath the flower head with stretched Forest Green crepe paper (see *Wrapping*).

BUDS

10. Poke short pieces of #22 wire into the small foam balls. Wrap them with Magenta crepe paper using the bow tie technique and wrap the stalk with stretched Forest Green crepe paper.

LEAVES

11. Prepare laminated Forest Green crepe paper and cut out leaf shapes using O5. Brush on soft pastels in browns to give your leaves a more realistic look.

FINAL ASSEMBLY

12. Position two to three buds at the top of a long piece of #18 wire and wrap them together with stretched Forest Green crepe paper.

13. Continue to wrap down the stalk, attaching the orchid blooms one by one. Bend the flower heads so that they face in various directions. Finally, attach the leaves with hot glue (see Tip).

14. For a striped orchid design, I like to add line details on each individual Blush Pink petal using a fine-tipped brush marker in dark pink or maroon.

When adding the leaves remember to have a few inches of bare wire at the bottom to anchor the blooms into the pot.

If you plan to 'pot' your orchid, make sure your wire stalk is long enough to hold the flower heads at the correct height.

Delphiniums

DIFFICULTY

Known for their stately, towering stalks, delphiniums are my go-to flower whenever I need a tall flowering element in my bouquets. The individual blooms are not necessarily difficult to make – in fact, they're pretty easy! However, you have to cut many small petals for a full tower, so it is crucial to arm yourself with patience when tackling this project. While I prefer my delphiniums in a purple blend, blues and pinks are also pretty colour options for delphiniums.

YOU WILL NEED

CREPE PAPER
- Dark Purple #593
- Violet #17E/2
- White #600
- Forest Green #561

OTHER MATERIALS
- Pre-wrapped #18 wire
- #24 and #26 wire
- Wooden skewer
- Scissors and wire cutters
- Mini hot glue gun
- White craft glue

TEMPLATES
Petals: DE1

Flower centre: DE2, DE3

Leaves: DE4

MAIN TECHNIQUES
Bow Ties, Cupping, Fringing, Laminating, Wrapping

BLOOMS

1. Cut a whole bunch of delphinium petals (using template DE1) from stretched Dark Purple and Violet crepe paper. To create a short tower, you would need approximately 22 blooms, which means you will need at least 220 petals (that's ten petals per small flower). For each petal, cup gently at their bellies.

2. Cut one of DE2 from stretched Dark Purple crepe paper and one of DE3 from stretched White crepe paper for each delphinium centre. Fringe each piece, snipping approximately three-quarters of its width.

3. Bend short pieces of #26 wire to serve as the individual flower stalks (I loop the wire to increase the surface area). With hot glue, wrap the fringed DE2 around the wire tip, followed by the fringed DE3 to create the centre of the flower.

4. Glue on ten cupped petals around the flower centre using hot glue – I suggest splitting the petals into two layers of five petals each. Remember to avoid gluing the petals back-to-back. As we have two shades of purple, we can mix the shades of petals within an individual bloom.

5. Wrap the individual bloom stalks under the flowerhead in stretched Forest Green crepe paper.

6. Keep in mind that for an ombre effect to your delphinium tower, you'll need to blend the two shades of purple so that the lighter shade is at the top and the darker shade at the bottom. I do this rather intuitively, and I make a few blooms in all Violet, a handful of blooms in all Dark Purple, and finally a bunch of blooms that have a mix of both purples that goes right in the middle of the stalk to transition between the two shades.

BUDS AND UNOPENED BLOOMS

7. For the smallest buds, use the bow tie technique and wrap Violet crepe paper around the tips of short lengths of #26 wire. Add three to four long Forest Green triangles around the wrapped portion as the sepals. For small, unopened blooms, add three DE1 petals in Violet around a wrapped wire tip. I like to make four buds and four small unopened blooms for one delphinium tower.

ASSEMBLING THE MAIN STALK

8. With stretched Forest Green crepe paper, start wrapping the smallest buds and the unopened blooms at the top of your pre-wrapped #18 wire.

9. Continue wrapping with the full blooms, remembering to create an ombre effect. To create a gentle tapering effect, extend the blooms further and further away from the main stalk towards the bottom. I fit three to four blooms in a round at the top, and gradually increase to five to six blooms in a round nearer to the bottom.

LEAVES

10. Delphinium leaves are rather complicated and I found that the easiest way to make them is to split each leaf into five sections. To make a leaf, you'll need six of DE4 from stretched Forest Green crepe paper. Take one DE4 leaf and spread a thin layer of white craft glue on its surface.

11. Next, add a long piece of #24 wire down its middle. Cover this wire with another piece of DE4. This laminated wired piece will be the centre of the completed leaf.

12. To create a palmate shape, I glue four DE4s overlapping each other in a fanned-out shape. I then glue the laminated wired DE4 piece right in the middle. I recommend using white craft glue instead of hot glue for this step.

13. To add dimension to the leaf, pinch the base of the leaf right under the middle, laminated piece and curl out the ends of the leaves with a wooden skewer. Wrap the wire right below the leaf with matching stretched Forest Green crepe paper strips for the petiole.

14. Make about six to eight leaves and wrap them under the blooms. The delphinium tower is very tall, so I recommend balancing out the base with a dense layer of leaves. You can also vary the size of the leaves.

I've created an ombre tower but you can also go for just one single colour or mix in even more shades.

Tulips

DIFFICULTY

These striking, striped tulips were very much inspired by my first trip to Amsterdam where tulips grow in abundance, even along the roadside! For this tutorial, I've kept the centre very simple since it will be mostly hidden anyway. On the other hand, the striped design on the petal is a little complicated and calls for fine cutting and gluing skills. To display them, I like potting two or three of these tulip stalks in a small pot, or they'll look good in a bouquet as well.

YOU WILL NEED

CREPE PAPER

- White #600
- Crimson Red #582
- Black #602
- Vanilla #577
- Forest Green #561

OTHER MATERIALS

- Pre-wrapped #18 wire
- #26 wire
- Wooden skewer
- Scissors and wire cutters
- White craft glue

TEMPLATES

Petals: T1, T2

Centre: T3

Leaves: T4

MAIN TECHNIQUES

Cupping, Curling, Laminating, Making Leaves

PETALS

1. I prefer my tulip petals to be wired so that they can hold an upright, rigid yet adjustable position, so I use the leaf-making technique on these petals. First, cut out triangles from stretched White crepe paper. Align the half-petal template T1 along the longest end of the triangle (using the lines on the template to guide you) and cut out two petal halves to make one petal. You will need six petals for one tulip (12 T1s in total).

2. Draw a line of white craft glue along the longest edge of one petal half. Place a short piece of #26 wire along this line and cover this wire with the other half of the petal by overlapping slightly.

3. Cut thin, long triangles from stretched Crimson Red crepe paper and glue one over the middle section of each petal. This helps to hide the wire too.

4. To add the curved striped patterns to the petals, first cut out several T2 shapes from stretched Crimson Red crepe paper. From each T2 shape, cut away narrow, slightly curved triangles along the longest edge, making sure the triangles all point downwards towards the base of the T2 shape. You can choose to use the entire T2 shape or cut it in half. I generally use one whole T2 on one side of the tulip petal, and half of a T2 on the other side for an asymmetrical design.

5. Once you're happy with your trimmed T2 designs, glue them directly on to your petal using white craft glue. Make sure all the narrow corners are glued on evenly.

6. Take your scissors and trim off any protruding portions.

7. After the glue has dried, we'll need to sculpt each petal. Gently cup each side of the petal by pinching the top and bottom and stretching that side out until a slight curve is formed. Repeat on the other side.

8. With a wooden skewer, curl the tips of each petal downwards, towards the back of the petal, to further accentuate the concave shape.

9. Once each petal is cupped and curled, bend the wire within each petal gently with your hands to form a sharp 'C' shape.

ASSEMBLY

10. For the tulip stamen, cut a small rectangle from Black crepe paper using T3. Fringe this strip, making thick strips about three-quarters of the width, and then twist each narrow strip to form rounded, noodle-like strips.

11. Wrap the tip of a pre-wrapped #18 wire with Vanilla crepe paper, using the bow tie technique. Next, glue the fringed black strip around this tulip stamen.

12. Next, prepare stretched Forest Green crepe paper strips for wrapping. Attach the petals one by one around the stamen with the wrapping technique. I tend to attach three petals for the first layer and three for the outermost layer.

13. For the leaves, cut out two T4 shapes from stretched Forest Green crepe paper for each leaf. I prefer the leaves to be wired like the petals, so I laminate the leaves. To do so, spread a thin layer of white glue on one T4, add a piece of #26 wire in the middle (with the end of the wire poking out from the base of the leaf to be attached to the main stalk), and then cover it with another piece of T4.

14. Sculpt the leaves by cupping the base of each leaf.

15. Wrap two to three leaves to the tulip stalk using stretched Forest Green crepe paper (see *Wrapping*). If you're planning on potting your tulips, remember to position the leaves higher up the stalk and leave a portion of the bottom stalk bare to be anchored into the pot.

Foxgloves

DIFFICULTY

With slinky, towering columns, sweet pastel shades and signature spots, foxgloves are definitely one of the more whimsical blooms in this book. Even the name recalls a magical, fairy-tale garden. For a beautiful ombre effect, I love blending cream, lilac and blush pink shades, but of course you are welcome to try other colours or have your entire stalk in just a single shade. I adore potting two foxglove stalks together, and I even have a pot on display on my nightstand!

YOU WILL NEED

CREPE PAPER
- Cream #603
- Lilac #592
- Blush Pink #17A3
- Light Green #562

OTHER MATERIALS
- Pre-wrapped #18 wire
- #26 wire
- Crepe paper scraps in Cream
- Soft pastels in browns
- White acrylic paint
- Paintbrush
- Maroon marker
- Wooden skewer
- Scissors and wire cutters
- Mini hot glue gun
- White craft glue

TEMPLATES
Petals: FOX1, FOX2

Calyx: FOX3

Leaves: FOX4

MAIN TECHNIQUES
Bow Ties, Cupping, Curling, Laminating

BLOOMS

1. Prepare laminated crepe paper in your chosen colours for the foxglove petals. I'm using a mix of Cream, Lilac and Blush Pink. For a small stalk, I usually need about 14 large petals (template FOX1) and 14 small petals (FOX2). Cup the bellies of all FOX1s and FOX2s.

2. With a wooden skewer, gently curl the tips of all FOX2s inwards.

3. Curl the top edges of the FOX1s backwards, again using a skewer.

4. For all FOX1s and only half of the FOX2s, paint an oval in the middle of each petal with white acrylic paint. I usually mix my acrylic paint with just a slight touch of water for a smooth painted oval.

5. Once the paint has dried, draw dots within the white oval with a maroon marker.

6. To wire each individual flower, prepare long pieces of #26 wire, bend each in half (to increase the surface area for wrapping), and wrap the tips using the bow tie technique with a matching colour of crepe paper.

7. For small blooms, glue one painted FOX2 and one non-painted FOX2 to the front and back of the wrapped wire tip using hot glue.

8. For large blooms, we will need to wrap FOX1 around itself so that it creates a trumpet shape with a slight overlap. Glue the ends together with white craft glue.

9. Once the glue has dried, poke a wrapped wire through the bottom of the FOX1 trumpet.

10. Give the base of FOX1 a good squeeze around the wrapped wire, making sure that it has a tight grasp around the wrapped portion of the wire. Add hot glue to seal it in place.

11. Cut a whole bunch of calyx shapes (FOX3) from stretched Light Green crepe paper and wrap them around the base of each bloom, again using hot glue.

BUDS

12. For the ombre effect, I like my foxglove buds to be Cream in colour. To make small round buds, I first roll crepe paper scraps (preferably in Cream) into tiny balls. I then wrap them inside a bow tie and attach them to a piece of #26 wire using hot glue. Wrap the base of each bud with a calyx shape (FOX3) as well.

ASSEMBLY

13. Starting at the top of a pre-wrapped #18 wire, wrap on the buds with stretched Light Green crepe paper strips, followed by the small blooms, and finally the large ones (see *Wrapping*). To achieve the classic conical shape, add more flowers per layer as you progress down the stalk.

14. To complete the stalk, make stretched Light Green leaves using FOX4 and colour them before adding to the stalk (see *Making Leaves*). I also like to attach thin narrow triangles in stretched Light Green in between the leaves along the main stalk for extra detail.

Succulents

DIFFICULTY

Knowing how to make crepe paper succulents is a must in every paper florist's arsenal. Despite having an unorthodox appearance, once you've mastered the special technique for making these thick, plump succulent leaves, you'll find that this project is possibly the easiest one in the book. As with many of the other projects, colouring the tips is optional, but I find that the additional colouring really makes a difference and helps to elevate the look of your succulent.

YOU WILL NEED

CREPE PAPER
- Teal Green #560

OTHER MATERIALS
- Pre-wrapped #18 wire
- Soft pastels in pink and red
- Paintbrush
- Scissors and wire cutters
- Mini hot glue gun

TEMPLATES
Leaves: SU1, SU2, SU3, SU4

MAIN TECHNIQUES
Bow Ties, Cupping

LEAVES

1. Using the templates, cut rectangles of Teal Green crepe paper in these quantities: three of SU1, five of SU2, six of SU3 and 12 of SU4.

2. For each rectangle, twist the upper half of the strip to the back. This creates a twisted knot in the middle, similar to what we do for the bow tie technique.

3. Pull down the top half so that it joins the bottom half of the strip, pressing them together so that the twisted knot is now right at the tip of your succulent leaf.

4. Cup both layers of the leaf by stretching out both sides right under the knotted tip, creating a wide, fat, dome-shaped leaf.

5. Glue the layers of each leaf together by adding a drop of hot glue in between the layers and pressing them together.

6. Trim off the two sharp corners at the bottom of each leaf to create a tapered base. You can trim more or less off depending on your preference, just try to make sure that the shape is generally consistent throughout all leaf sizes.

ASSEMBLY

7. Now, let's attach the leaves to our wire, working from the smallest to the largest. First, glue on one SU1 leaf around the tip of a short pre-wrapped #18 wire, making sure it is wrapped tightly and that the wire tip is hidden. I use hot glue for all my leaves so I can work quickly. Then, glue on the other two SU1 leaves to the front and back of the first leaf.

8. Glue on the five medium sized leaves (SU2) in a round as the second layer.

9. For the third layer, glue on six SU3 leaves in a round.

10. I like to divide my largest leaves into two layers: six SU4 leaves for layer 4 and six SU4 leaves for layer 5. As much as possible, avoid gluing the leaves directly back-to-back, as this can cause some leaves to be hidden.

11. If you find it hard to glue on the leaves for the last layer as our succulent has grown bulkier, I suggest flipping the succulent over and working on it while it is upside down. This will make it easier for you to attach any new leaves.

12. Once you've added all your leaves, have a quick check of the top view to ensure there are no obvious gaps.

13. To add colour, cup the succulent in one hand and gently squeeze the leaves tightly together – this makes it easier to rub on soft pastels onto the tips of each leaf. I recommend picking a bright, contrasting colour to highlight the tips of the leaves. You may wish to mix two or more colours.

14. Once you are satisfied with the soft pastels application, blend the colours with a paintbrush.

I've used a teal green for this tutorial, but this succulent looks great in any shade of green. If you're adventurous, why not try blue, pink or reds?

How to Pot Your Plants

Potting your crepe paper creations is a great way to display them around the house or even present them as gifts. Here, I share my method of using floral foam that's widely available at most wholesale florists. If you prefer to use an alternative medium, you could explore using small pebbles or chicken wires inside your pot.

YOU WILL NEED

- Floral foam
- Newspaper
- Knife
- Pot (preferably without drain holes)
- Shredded paper (used for packaging and gifts)

1. Floral foam generates dust, so before you begin, it's a good idea to protect your table with a plastic covering or a sheet of newspaper. Choose your pot and cut the foam with the knife according to the pot's size. Make sure to cut the foam slightly larger than the base of the pot, so that it will fit snugly.

2. Forcefully squish the foam block into your pot, making sure it fits tightly by pressing down with your fingers. Discard any bits and pieces of the foam that fall off.

3. Poke in the stalk of your crepe paper bloom and use shredded paper to hide the floral foam. I generally use brown shredded paper to give the impression of soil.

1.

2.

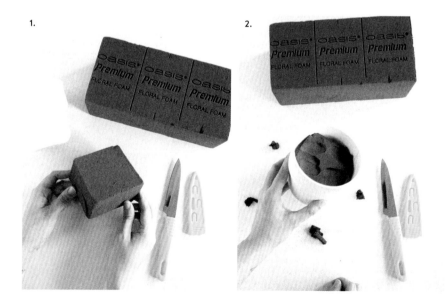

3.

TEMPLATES

All templates are full-size. You can download printable versions of these templates from: www.davidandcharles.com

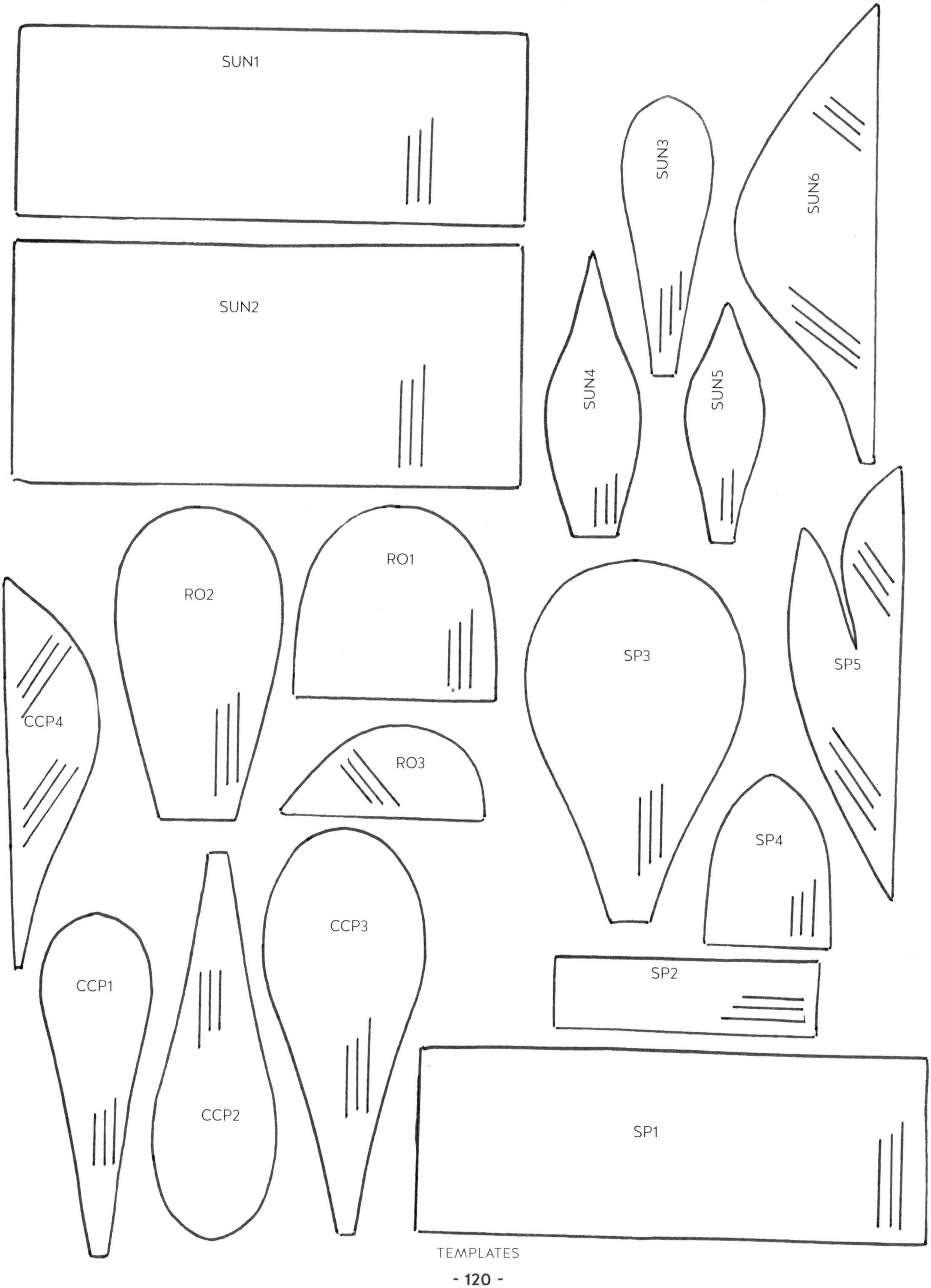

SUN1

SUN2

SUN3

SUN6

SUN4

SUN5

RO1

RO2

CCP4

RO3

SP3

SP5

SP4

CCP1

CCP3

CCP2

SP2

SP1

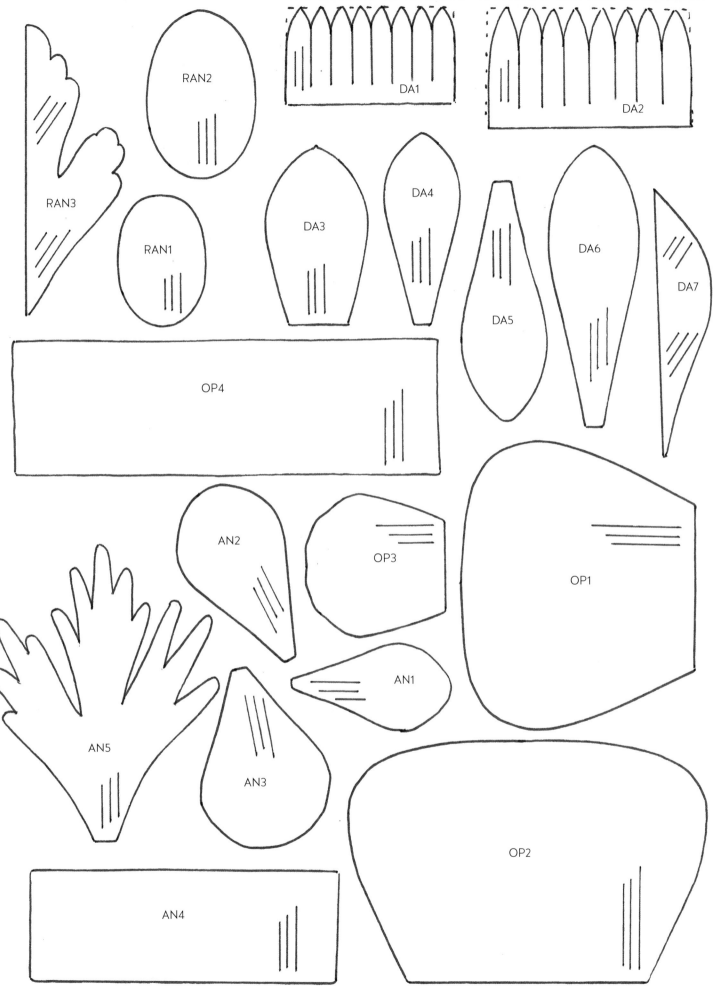

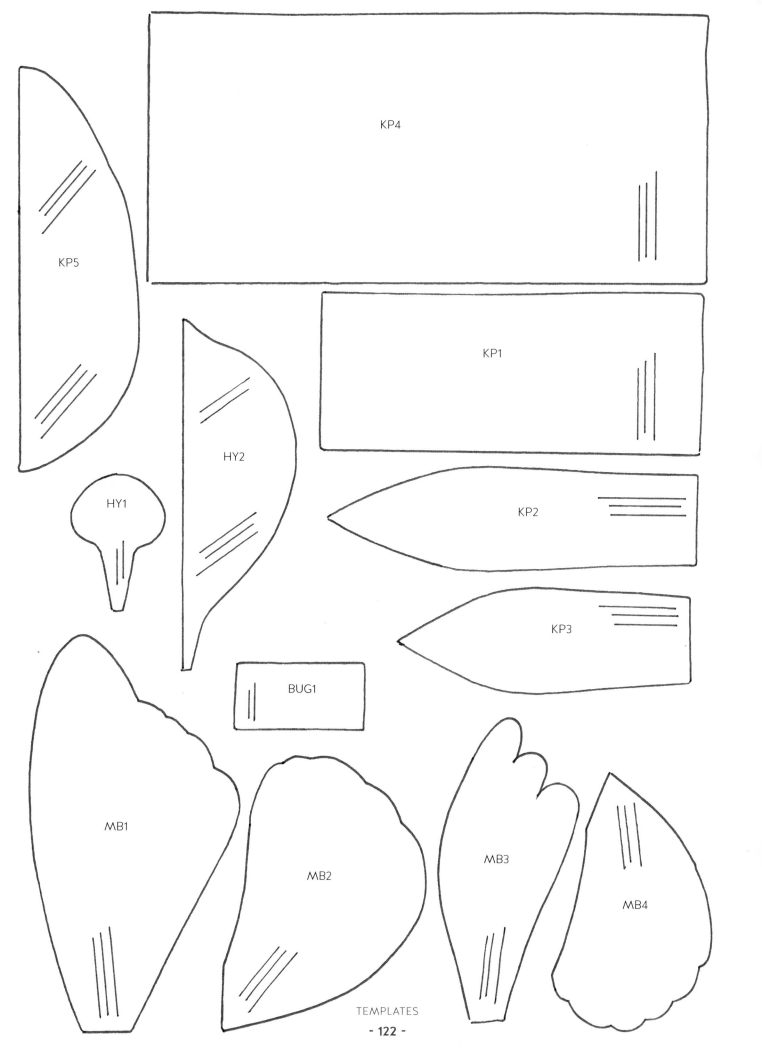

KP4

KP5

KP1

HY2

HY1

KP2

KP3

BUG1

MB1

MB2

MB3

MB4

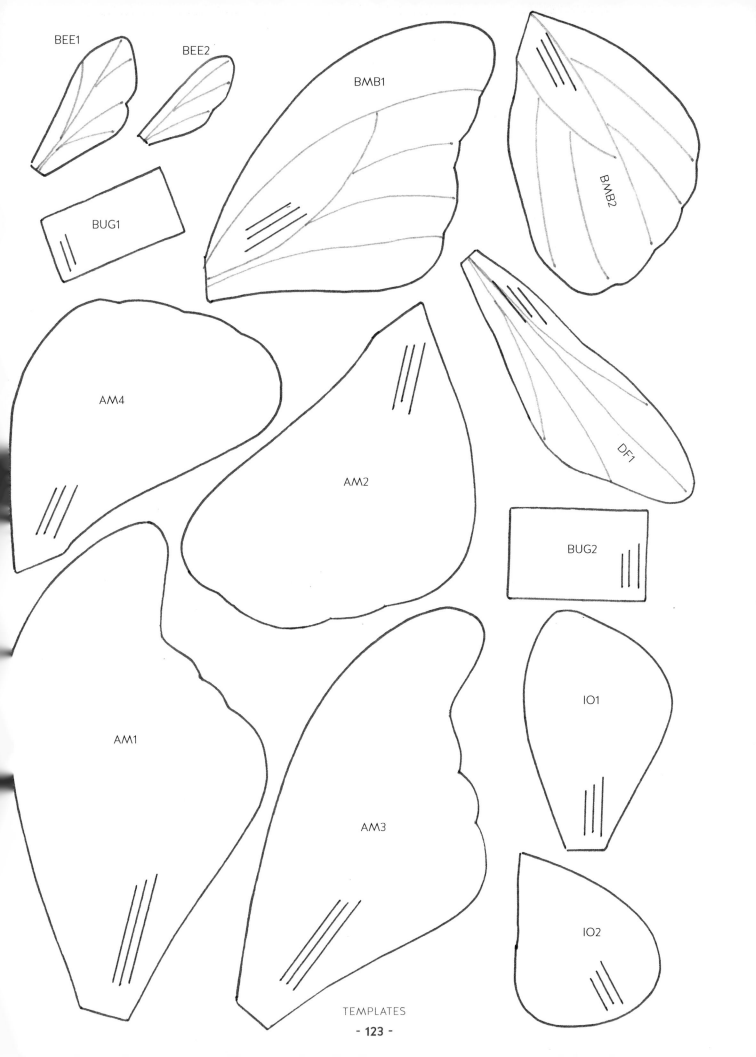

BEE1

BEE2

BMB1

BMB2

BUG1

AM4

AM2

DF1

BUG2

IO1

AM1

AM3

IO2

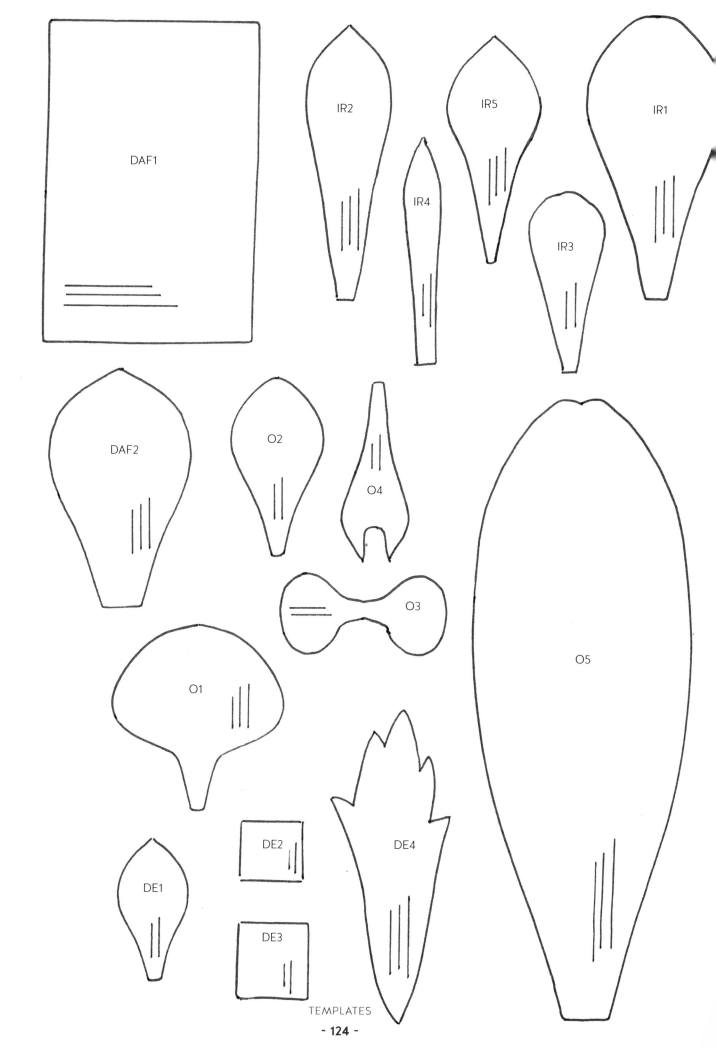

DAF1

IR2

IR5

IR1

IR4

IR3

DAF2

O2

O4

O5

O3

O1

DE1

DE2

DE4

DE3

ACKNOWLEDGEMENTS

First and foremost, I am indebted to my parents for their unwavering support and constant guidance. They have more faith and confidence in me than I sometimes have in myself, and they never once told me to give up on my dreams. This book would not have been possible without them!

A shout-out to my big brother Aaron and sister-in-law Wileen for always having my back. Not forgetting my new baby nephew Alexander, who has brought me many precious moments of joy and laughter in between the long hours that went into writing this book.

Much love to my friends who cheered me on, I treasure every world of encouragement you have given me!

I am so grateful for the amazing publishing team at David and Charles for helping me make a dream come true. A special thank you to Ame Verso, Sam Staddon, Jessica Cropper, Lucy Waldron, Ali Stark, Beverley Richardson, Clare Ashton and Claire Coakley for all your time and hard work!

I would be remiss if I did not mention some of the artists and mentors who have generously showered me with love and advice throughout my paper flower journey: Margie Keates, Jessie Chui, Kate Alarcon, Quynh Nguyen, Natalie Png, Kristen Kiong, Michelle Tan, the list goes on. Sending love to all of you.

To my loyal followers, students and fellow paper artists from all over the world – you have shown me more love than I probably deserve, you are the best!

To Daddy God, who at one of my lowest moments, gave me the vision for this book, and then gave me the courage, strength and wisdom to pursue it. I am so blessed.

And of course, to you, my reader, for purchasing this book. I look forward to seeing your wonderful creations.

Keep Blooming,

Eileen

ABOUT THE AUTHOR

Eileen is the cheerful paper artist behind her colourful online moniker Miss Petal & Bloom. She is based in Singapore and has been crafting whimsical crepe paper blooms since 2015. As a full-time paper florist, she has worked for brands such as Bvlgari Parfums, Jo Malone, The Body Shop, Chaumet, Keds, Coach, Olivia Burton, Harper's Bazaar Singapore and many more. Eileen is fully self-taught and hopes to spread the joy of crepe paper blooms and bugs to anyone with a passion for crafting! You can follow her vibrant paper flower journey on Instagram @misspetalandbloom.

INDEX

A DAVID AND CHARLES BOOK

© David and Charles, Ltd 2022

David and Charles is an imprint of David and Charles, Ltd
Suite A, Tourism House, Pynes Hill, Exeter, EX2 5WS

Text and Designs © Eileen Lim 2022
Layout and Photography © David and Charles, Ltd 2022

First published in the UK and USA in 2022

ISBN-13: 9781446309179 paperback
ISBN-13: 9781446381588 EPUB
ISBN-13: 9781446381571 PDF

This book has been printed on paper from approved suppliers and made from pulp from sustainable sources.

Printed in the UK by Buxton Press for:
David and Charles, Ltd
Suite A, Tourism House, Pynes Hill, Exeter, EX2 5WS

10 9 8 7 6 5 4 3 2 1

Publishing Director: Ame Verso
Editor: Jessica Cropper
Project Editors: Clare Ashton and Claire Coakley
Designer: Sam Staddon
Pre-press Designer: Ali Stark
Photography: Eileen Lim
Production Manager: Beverley Richardson

David and Charles publishes high-quality books on a wide range of subjects. For more information visit www.davidandcharles.com.

Share your makes with us on social media using #dandcbooks and follow us on Facebook and Instagram by searching for @dandcbooks.

Layout of the digital edition of this book may vary depending on reader hardware and display settings.